W9-BLY-923

BIBLIOPHILE
DIVERSE SPINES

Jane loves these books.
Some of Jamise's favorites!
MICHI
THE FIFTH SEASON N.K. JEMISIN
HELEN OYEYEMI Gingerbread
JOHNSON YOU SHOULD SEE ME IN A CROWN
THE GOD OF SMALL THINGS ARUNDHATI ROY
PACHINKO Min Jin Lee
EMPIRE OF WILD CHERIE DIMALINE
AMERICANAH CHIMAMANDA NGOZI ADICHIE
GOOD TALK MIRA JACOB
ISABEL ALLENDE THE HOUSE OF THE SPIRITS
SHARKS IN THE TIME OF SAVIORS | KAWAI STRONG WASHBURN
the changeling victor lavalle
THE OLD DRIFT NAMWALI SERPELL
A SUITABLE BOY VIKRAM SETH 20th ANNIVERSARY EDITION
MEN WE REAPED JESMYN WARD
Yaa Gyasi Homegoing
THE STREET ANN PETRY
The Fire Next Time James Baldwin
YRSA DALEY-WARD bone
NATIVE SON RICHARD WRIGHT
THE AUTOBIOGRAPHY OF MALCOLM X AS TOLD TO ALEX HALEY
Just Mercy Bryan Stevenson
SUGAR BERNICE L. McFADDEN
A KNOCK AT MIDNIGHT BRITTANY K. BARNETT
CLAUDIA RANKINE CITIZEN
THE WARMTH OF OTHER SUNS ISABEL WILKERSON
MAYA ANGELOU I KNOW WHY THE CAGED BIRD SINGS

BIBLIOPHILE
DIVERSE SPINES

---

by Jamise Harper & Jane Mount

illustrated by Jane Mount

CHRONICLE BOOKS

SAN FRANCISCO

Library of Congress Cataloging-in-Publication Data available.

ISBN 978-1-7972-1191-6

Manufactured in Italy.

Design by Kristen Hewitt.

10 9 8 7 6 5 4 3 2 1

Chronicle books and gifts are available at special quantity discounts to corporations, professional associations, literacy programs, and other organizations. For details and discount information, please contact our premiums department at corporatesales@chroniclebooks.com or at 1-800-759-0190.

Chronicle Books LLC
680 Second Street
San Francisco, California 94107
www.chroniclebooks.com

For marginalized writers and readers, and for the booksellers, librarians, and booklovers who champion those voices.

CONTENTS

INTRODUCTION

In creating this miscellany, our goal is for you to find at least ten new-to-you and irresistible diverse books by authors of backgrounds different from your own (or from your own that you haven't yet read!), that you'll read in the next year. And then ten more for the year after that, and so on. The idea is to keep seeking out and reading diverse stories. Think of it as your very own pocket-sized (well, if you have a large pocket) local bookstore full of passionate shelftalkers from people with all different experiences.

The authors, illustrators, designers, store owners, and bookstagrammers highlighted in this book are all Black, Indigenous, and people of color, most existing in spaces where they have been marginalized by a dominant white society. There are, of course, many other ways to define diversity, but this is the one we have embraced for this book. It is our small offering to the world, sparked by social injustices and racial reckonings, and inspired by many years of reading diversely and realizing what magic can happen when people leave their comfort zones.

Reading diverse stories exposes us to other people's experiences and expands our awareness of other cultures. Living several hours vicariously through a protagonist different from your own race helps foster empathy and gives you a look at life through a different lens. Reading won't solve all problems, of course, and you can never fully walk in another person's shoes, but it offers a brilliant path to greater understanding and opens up pathways for conversations. Plus, it's just more interesting to read broadly, to discover stories about other ways to exist, other worlds to inhabit. In the end, you may find that the characters in these stories have the same loves and struggles you do.

To paraphrase what professor and children's literature scholar Rudine Sims Bishop wrote (about children, particularly, but it works for everyone), books can be windows and sliding doors that you can walk through to immerse yourself in new worlds, but should also be mirrors, so you can see yourself reflected back. Representation does matter, and if you don't see it, you won't realize you can be it. Reading books about people like yourself—especially if you're part of a marginalized group—gifts you the sense of belonging, which is crucial to a happy life.

Before we dive in, a little about us:

Jamise grew up with a book always in hand, and as an adult, most of the time has a glass of wine in the other. She loves talking about both, and friends always ask her for recommendations. In 2015, she joined Instagram, and at her sister's suggestion, began sharing the books she read and pairing them with wine, as @spinesvines. While she reads widely, she centers her focus on Black women and women of color. This led her to create #diversespines and then later @diversespines, to help readers diversify their bookshelves. A champion for amplifying marginalized voices, Jamise passionately believes that reading diversely cultivates the opportunity for growth and understanding.

Jane, too, grew up with a book in hand, and a paintbrush in the other (making it hard to hold the wine at times, but she figures it out). She has been drawing books since 2008, when she first realized how lovely they look together and how passionate booklovers are about them. Since then, she has created more than four thousand commissioned pieces, each filled with a person's absolute, heart-changing, happy-tears-making favorite books. The most important thing she has learned is that any book, read at the right time, can change everything, and that reading truly makes the world a better place.

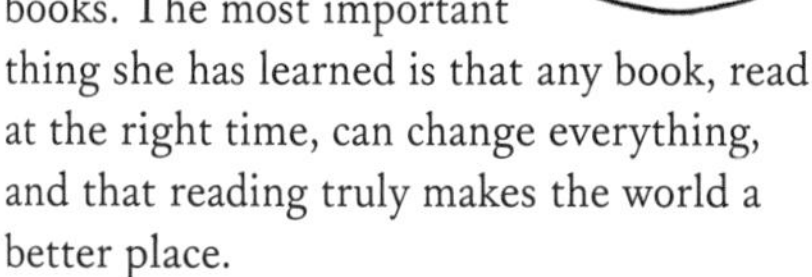

We met soon after Jamise's son AJ commissioned Jane to create a mug full of diverse spines for Jamise's Christmas present in 2018. We chatted after that, but had never worked together before creating this book, nor even spoken on the phone. As we live far apart and were making this book in the midst of a pandemic, we collaborated remotely for the entire process and are both amazed at how easy and enjoyable it was, despite the crazy deadlines.

We've included hundreds of books inside this book with a bit of information on many of them, but there is so much more that could be said about each, so just know they are *all* worth reading. And there are (of course!) *so many more* books we wish we could have squeezed in. Please don't feel limited by our lists; keep exploring on your own and dive into the vast number of wonderful books out there by authors from diverse backgrounds.

On the other hand, if the idea of adding hundreds of books to your To Be Read pile seems overwhelming, don't worry! On the opposite page is a stack of brilliant books, and that is where you can start. They are some of our favorites: some classics by legends and some fresh, urgent voices.

You will notice throughout the book we have added short comments here and there. For reference, this is Jamise's handwriting and this is Jane's.

The Fire Next Time James Baldwin
Just Mercy Bryan Stevenson
ALICE WALKER THE COLOR PURPLE
INTERIOR CHINATOWN CHARLES YU
Disability Visibility EDITED BY Alice Wong
KIM JOHNSON THIS IS MY AMERICA
NEVER LET ME GO KAZUO ISHIGURO
Trick Mirror Jia Tolentino
EMPIRE OF WILD CHERIE DIMALINE
SISTER OUTSIDER AUDRE LORDE
AMERICANAH CHIMAMANDA NGOZI ADICHIE
INVISIBLE MAN RALPH ELLISON
TAYARI JONES AN AMERICAN MARRIAGE
CLAUDIA RANKINE CITIZEN Graywolf Press
HOW WE FIGHT FOR OUR LIVES SAEED JONES
IF THEY COME FOR US FATIMAH ASGHAR
MINOR FEELINGS CATHY PARK HONG
ACEVEDO THE POET X
INFINITE COUNTRY PATRICIA ENGEL
MAYA ANGELOU I KNOW WHY THE CAGED BIRD SINGS
ONE HUNDRED YEARS OF SOLITUDE
MARCH LEWIS AYDIN POWELL
THE JOY LUCK CLUB AMY TAN PUTNAM
MACHADO IN THE DREAM HOUSE
ERIKA L. SÁNCHEZ I AM NOT YOUR PERFECT MEXICAN DAUGHTER KNOPF
ISABEL ALLENDE THE HOUSE OF THE SPIRITS
THOMAS THE HATE U GIVE
TA-NEHISI COATES BETWEEN THE WORLD AND ME
AN AMERICAN SUNRISE JOY HARJO
CEREMONY LESLIE MARMON SILKO Viking
SING, UNBURIED, SING JESMYN WARD
WHITE TEETH ZADIE SMITH VINTAGE
SANDRA CISNEROS THE HOUSE ON MANGO STREET
KHALED HOSSEINI THE KITE RUNNER
PACHINKO Min Jin Lee
GOOD TALK MIRA JACOB
OCTAVIA E. BUTLER KINDRED
THE VANISHING HALF BRIT BENNETT
THEIR EYES WERE WATCHING GOD ZORA NEALE HURSTON
THE FIFTH SEASON N.K. JEMISIN
HEAVY KIESE LAYMON
JOHNSON ALL BOYS AREN'T BLUE FSG
JASON REYNOLDS LONG WAY DOWN
LOT BRYAN WASHINGTON
STAMPED FROM THE BEGINNING The Definitive History of Racist Ideas in America Ibram X. Kendi
JOHNSON YOU SHOULD SEE ME IN A CROWN
THE COMPLETE PERSEPOLIS Marjane Satrapi PANTHEON
BELOVED Toni Morrison VINTAGE
BECOMING – MICHELLE OBAMA CROWN
HARUKI MURAKAMI THE WIND-UP BIRD CHRONICLE
Langston Hughes Selected Poems Vintage
Yaa Gyasi Homegoing Knopf
THE GOD OF SMALL THINGS ARUNDHATI ROY RANDOM HOUSE
KIMMERER BRAIDING SWEETGRASS
Ocean Vuong On Earth We're Briefly Gorgeous Penguin Press
AGAINST THE LOVELESS WORLD SUSAN ABULHAWA
There There Tommy Orange
BLESS ME, ULTIMA RUDOLFO ANAYA
The NICKEL BOYS COLSON WHITEHEAD
CALLENDER FELIX EVER AFTER
NIC STONE Dear Martin CROWN
SHARKS IN THE TIME OF SAVIORS KAWAI STRONG WASHBURN
THE SECRET LIVES OF CHURCH LADIES PHILYAW
SABRINA & CORINA KALI FAJARDO-ANSTINE
THE WEDDING DATE JASMINE GUILLORY
CHANG-RAE LEE NATIVE SPEAKER
THE WARMTH OF OTHER SUNS ISABEL WILKERSON RANDOM HOUSE
THE ROUND HOUSE A Novel LOUISE ERDRICH
NATIVE SON RICHARD WRIGHT HARPER

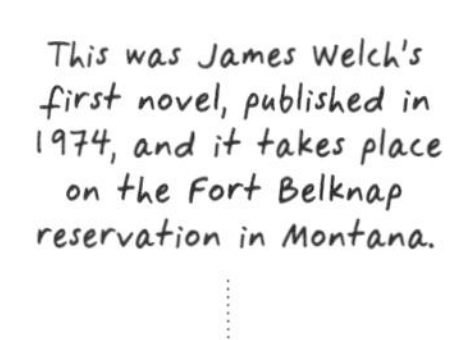

Jamaica Kincaid's coming-of-age story of a girl growing apart from her mother in Antigua

"Beloved" won the Pulitzer Prize for fiction in 1988, and was made into a movie starring Oprah Winfrey, Danny Glover, Thandiwe Newton, and Kimberly Elise.

THE SOULS OF BLACK FOLK BY W.E.B DUBOIS

BLESS ME, ULTIMA RUDOLFO ANAYA

A House for Mr Biswas V.S. Naipaul McGraw-Hill

JEAN TOOMER CANE

THE STREET ANN PETRY

COELHO The Alchemist

THE AUTOBIOGRAPHY OF MALCOLM X AS TOLD TO ALEX HALEY

THINGS FALL APART Anchor Books Chinua Achebe

SANDRA CISNEROS THE HOUSE ON MANGO STREET VINTAGE

a raisin in the sun Lorraine Hansberry RANDOM HOUSE

FICCIONES BY JORGE LUIS BORGES GROVE PRESS

THE PROPHET • KAHLIL GIBRAN KNOPF

GLORIA NAYLOR THE WOMEN OF BREWSTER PLACE VIKING

Pedro Páramo Juan Rulfo GROVE PRESS

PENGUIN VITAE PASSING | NELLA LARSEN

BOOKER T. WASHINGTON Up from Slavery

NATIVE SON RICHARD WRIGHT HARPERS

Narrative of the Life of FREDERICK DOUGLASS, an American Slave

With over 80 million copies sold worldwide, this story of Santiago, an Andalusian shepherd boy, and his search for happiness, is considered a masterpiece.

Inspired by Thomas-Alexandre Dumas, the son of a Black slave, who rose to great heights during the French Revolution and became the first Black general in the French army

The first script by a Black woman to be performed on Broadway, and a poignant survival story of an African American family living in Chicago's South Side during the segregated 1950s

THE DEATH OF ARTEMIO CRUZ Carlos Fuentes

ALEXANDRE DUMAS • THE COUNT OF MONTE CRISTO FOLIO

OKADA NO NO BOY LITTLE

CLASSICS

Rich in history and timeless storytelling, classics speak to interconnected human experiences that have stood the test of time and are still meaningful today.

Anchor 2008 paperback, design by Helen Yentus, art by Edel Rodriguez

Things Fall Apart celebrated its 60th anniversary in 2018. The novel has sold over 20 million copies and has been translated into over 57 languages. President Barack Obama called Achebe's novel "A true classic of world literature . . . A masterpiece that has inspired generations of writers in Nigeria, across Africa, and around the world."

Ann Petry's 1946 debut novel, *The Street*, was the first novel by an African American woman to sell more than a million copies. The story follows the daily struggles of Lucite Johnson, a Black single mother of an eight-year-old son, striving for the "American Dream" amid racism, poverty, and the violent streets of Harlem.

Mariner 2020 paperback, art by Nathan Burton

← Petry was a registered pharmacist prior to becoming a journalist, novelist, and short story and children's book writer.

Claude McKay was ahead of his time when he wrote *Romance in Marseille* in 1930. It is one of the earliest African American queer fiction stories covering radical politics, racial identity, and sexual preference. Ninety years after he wrote this bold novel, it was published for the first time in 2020. McKay was a pioneering figure in the Harlem Renaissance, and his poetry book *Harlem Shadows* was a strong influence on the movement.

Penguin Classics 2020 paperback art by Sean Qualls

Vintage 1991 paperback, art by Edel Rodriguez

Published over 35 years ago, *The House on Mango Street* has sold over 6 million copies and has been translated into over 20 languages. This coming-of-age classic about Esperanza Cordero, a young Chicana girl growing up in Chicago, is required reading for many educational institutions. Asked if it's autobiographical, Sandra Cisneros states, "I'm not Esperanza but I'm the sum of all stories that have passed through me, that I've heard, that I've witnessed and Esperanza becomes a composite of all of the above."

LEGENDS

JAMES BALDWIN

(1924–1987)

Go Tell It on the Mountain

Hailed as his finest work, Baldwin's first published novel is semi-autobiographical. The main character's struggles with family, religion, race, and sex emulated Baldwin's life.

Knopf 1953 hardcover, art by John O'Hara Cosgrave

LESLIE MARMON SILKO

(1948–)

Ceremony

Penguin Classics 2006 paperback, design by Peter Mendelsund, photo by Didier Gaillard

Silko's first novel examines the post-war trauma of a Native American soldier who fought against the Japanese and was captured during World War II.

SANDRA CISNEROS

(1954–)

Woman Hollering Creek and Other Stories

Vintage 1992 paperback, design by Susan Shapiro, art by Nivia Gonzalez

Cisneros gives voice to women who are often silenced. This short-story collection centers the struggles of different generations of women, human interaction, and Chicana culture.

Vintage 2000 paperback, design by John Gall

HARUKI MURAKAMI

(1949–)

Norwegian Wood

Norwegian Wood is a coming-of-age story about students navigating through love, depression, suicide, and grief. It is hailed as Murakami's most autobiographical book of fiction.

ISABEL ALLENDE

(1942–)

Eva Luna

Dial Press 2005 paperback

Known for her signature weaving together of magical realism and myth, Allende is one of the most widely read Spanish-language authors in the world.

Knopf 1934 hardcover

LANGSTON HUGHES

(1902–1967)

The Ways of White Folks

A central figure in the Harlem Renaissance, Hughes wrote a collection of fourteen short stories that focuses on the objectification of Black people and their everyday encounters with white people.

Amistad 2020 hardcover, design by Stephen Brayda, art by Bradley Theodore

ZORA NEALE HURSTON

(1891–1960)

Hitting a Straight Lick with a Crooked Stick: Stories from the Harlem Renaissance

Hurston is regarded as one the most prominent leaders of the Harlem Renaissance. This collection features 21 short stories, including 8 "lost" stories, showcasing African American culture, race, love, and Harlem.

TONI MORRISON

(1931–2019)

The Bluest Eye

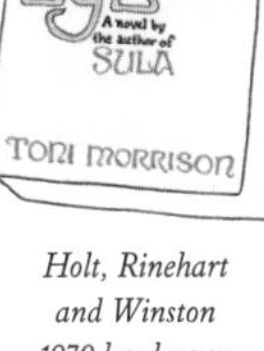

Holt, Rinehart and Winston 1970 hardcover, design by Holly McNeely-Poindexter

The first novel written by Morrison introduces readers to Pecola Breedlove, a young Black girl who prays for her eyes to turn blue because she believes they will make her beautiful.

TURN OF THE CENTURY FICTION

The end of one millennium and the beginning of the next is really just one more day after another, but for this last one, we humans freaked out a bit: first partying "like it's 1999," and then panicking over Y2K, and finally settling into the sobering new reality of a war on terror and a recession. These books span the years from 1990 to 2009, twenty years of immense change.

As a young boy growing up in Kabul, Khaled Hosseini loved to fly kites with his cousins and friends. After watching a 1999 news report about the Taliban regime banning Afghan people from flying kites, he felt compelled to write a short story. A few years later he rediscovered the short story in storage in his garage and it became the inspiration for his first novel, *The Kite Runner*.

Vintage 2006 paperback, design by Jamie Keenan, photo by Gabrielle Rever/ Getty Images

Never Let Me Go is a lovely, heartbreaking book, all about what it is to be human and mortal, and it was made into a lovely, heartbreaking film starring Carey Mulligan, Keira Knightley, and Andrew Garfield. When asked about the balance between the novel's sadness and hope, author Kazuo Ishiguro said, "You know, the fact is, yes, we will all fade away and die, but people can find the energy to create, you know, little pockets of happiness and decency while we're here."

Like his character Chino in *Bodega Dreams*, Ernesto Quiñonez grew up on the streets in Spanish Harlem. About the audience for his novel, he said, "There are many who still say: 'Latinos don't read.' I don't believe that for a minute. What happened is that, for a very long time, publishing didn't do enough to create the market for them. The more mainstream houses didn't bring out enough novels or nonfiction books that Latinos could relate to. Only now has the industry started to take notice that there is an audience—a diverse and eager market—for books that appeal to Latinos."

Vintage 2015 paperback, design by Perry De La Vega

In the Time of the Butterflies is a fictional account of real people in history, the four Mirabal sisters (Patria, Minerva, María Teresa, and Dedé), revolutionary activists in the Dominican Republic during the dictatorship of Rafael Trujillo. Three of the sisters were assassinated in 1960. Julia Alvarez spent her first ten years in the Dominican Republic, until her father's involvement in the same rebellion against El Jefe forced them to flee.

The Mirabal sisters' code name was "Las Mariposas," Spanish for "the butterflies."

Rohinton Mistry's second novel is set in 1975 during the turmoil of "The Emergency" declared across India by Prime Minister Indira Gandhi.

"Native Speaker" won the 1996 PEN/Hemingway Award for Debut Novel.

One of my favorite books of all time! It begins with a missing cat.

The story of four African American girlfriends navigating love and life. A 1995 movie version was directed by Forest Whitaker, starring Whitney Houston, Angela Bassett, Loretta Devine, and Lela Rochon.

Smith's debut novel, covering 150 years of history and traversing through multiple continents

Lisa See is the great-granddaughter of a Chinese man and a white woman who defied racist laws to marry in 1890s Los Angeles.

EDITIONS

Zora Neale Hurston's *Their Eyes Were Watching God* was first published in 1937 to mixed reviews and low retail sales. At the time, novelist Richard Wright criticized it for its "facile sensuality" and Ralph Ellison for its "blight of calculated burlesque." But by the 1970s (well after Hurston's death in 1960), a new audience discovered Hurston's genius (with some help from Alice Walker, who wrote a brilliant 1975 essay in *Ms.* magazine called "Looking for Zora"). Janie Crawford's recounting of her life, her loves, and a hurricane is now considered one of the most influential novels of all time. Walker once wrote, "There is no book more important to me than this one," and Zadie Smith said, "There is no novel I love more," while Oprah Winfrey declared it her "favorite love story of all time." Many different editions have been published in the last 80-plus years, and here are several.

J. B. Lippincott
1937
hardcover

The very first edition, with a dust jacket featuring the storm

University of Illinois Press
1978
paperback

This was the 50th anniversary edition.

HarperCollins
1990
paperback,
design by
Suzanne Noli,
art by
David Díaz

Harper
Perennial
2003
paperback

Harper Perennial 2006 paperback

In 2005, Oprah Winfrey produced a television film version for ABC, directed by Darnell Martin and starring Halle Berry, and new editions of the book have been published more frequently ever since.

Virago Modern Classics UK 2008 hardcover, art by Loïs Mailou Jones

Jones was an artist working in the United States and France during the Harlem Renaissance and up until her death in 1998 at age 92.

Amistad 2010 paperback, design by Milan Bozic

HarperCollins 2013 paperback

This was the 75th anniversary edition!

Tong won the V&A Illustration Award for Book Cover Design in 2019 for the Virago Modern Classics 40th Anniversary Series, which includes this cover.

Virago Modern Classics UK 2018, design by Yehrin Tong

Amistad 2021 paperback, design by Stephen Brayda, art by Patrick Dougher

In his work, artist Dougher "seeks to inspire and to celebrate the noble beauty and divine nature of people of African descent and to connect urban African American culture to its roots in sacred African art, spirituality, and ritual."

BELOVED BOOKSTORES

LOYALTY BOOKSTORE

Silver Spring, Maryland, USA / Washington, DC, USA
Instagram: @loyaltybooks

What began as a pop-up shop has since become one of the most treasured bookstores in the Washington, DC, area. Loyalty Bookstore, now with locations in downtown Silver Spring, Maryland, and in the Petworth neighborhood of Washington, DC, is owned by Hannah Oliver Depp, a Black and queer bookseller who has spent her career working to diversify the book industry in order for it to better serve the powerful communities of color and queerness. At Loyalty, they focus on centering traditionally marginalized voices by providing bookseller-curated books, gifts, and events to their intersectional community.

CAFE CON LIBROS

Brooklyn, New York, USA
Instagram: @cafeconlibros_bk

Cafe con Libros (coffee with books) is a feminist bookstore located in Crown Heights, Brooklyn. When store owner Kalima DeSuze opened it in 2017, she knew that she wanted a space that was explicitly feminist. Along with being able to enjoy a nice latte, customers can browse shelves filled with books written by womxn for womxn. The store also offers a monthly book subscription called "Feminist & Bookish," intersectional feminist books by, for, and about womxn and girls, that is mailed directly to the reader's home. DeSuze affirms that "the heart and soul of our industry is the spaces that we create in our communities—the spaces of learning, the spaces of action, community building, friendship building, and exchanging of ideas."

MARCUS BOOKS

Oakland, California, USA
Instagram: @marcus.books

Marcus Books is the oldest independent Black bookstore in the country. The bookstore's founders, Doctors Raye and Julian Richardson met while attending Tuskegee University, and in 1960, they founded Marcus Books (named after political activist and author Marcus Garvey). The store opened during the Black power movement, which then led to the Civil Rights Movement. For the past 60 years, the bookstore has become a literary and cultural hallmark serving the Black community in the Bay Area with books by and about African Americans. They have hosted iconic authors including Toni Morrison, Rosa Parks, Muhammad Ali, Maya Angelou, Walter Mosley, Angela Davis, and Nikki Giovanni; and Malcom X was one of the shop's customers. Today the store is owned and operated by the founders' children, Blanche Richardson, Billy Richardson, and Karen Johnson.

Everyone in the land of Popisho is born with a magical ability, called their "cors."

A brilliant book you really must read. Or listen to! The audiobook is narrated by Adjoa Andoh, a British stage and television actress who could make the dictionary sound thrilling.

Tommy Orange is a citizen of the Cheyenne and Arapaho Nations of Oklahoma, and his book is set in Oakland, California, where he grew up.

Longlisted for the 2019 National Book Award for Fiction, poet Ocean Vuong's debut novel is a son's letter to his mother who cannot read.

A coming-of-age story about Niru, a young Black male seeking to balance the expectations of his privileged Nigerian family while grappling with his sexuality and identity

The teen girls on a struggling high school field hockey team in 1980s Massachusetts turn to witchcraft.

Winner of the 2019 National Book Award for Fiction

CONTEMPORARY FICTION

The saying that "art imitates life" rings true in these modern stories representing real-life issues and societal problems. These stories center the gaze on authentic human experiences where fictionalized characters learn more about themselves, others, and our ever-changing world.

The first books that Bryan Washington took to and read were cookbooks. In 2017, he started writing on food websites about meals—achiote and yaka mein for *The Awl*, broth for *Hazlitt*. Before Washington's debut novel, *Memorial*, was published, he landed a television deal and a Good Morning America book club selection for it. His first book *Lot,* a short-story collection, was featured on President Barack Obama's favorite books of 2019 and the National Book Foundation's 5 Under 35 list.

Yaka mein is a rich beef noodle soup popular in New Orleans.

One World 2020 hardcover, design and art by Donna Cheng

After a successful career as a legal academic, Ingrid Persaud began writing in her forties. She describes *Love After Love* as "a love letter from self-exile to home, but without denying the very real problems of crime and governance." If she were stranded on a desert island and could only read one short story ever again, Persaud would read *Chronicle of a Death Foretold* by Gabriel García Márquez.

Angie Kim first thought about writing after she became a mother and all three of her kids were having issues that required several hospital visits. Being a Korean immigrant, former trial lawyer, and the mother of a real-life hyperbaric oxygen therapy ("submarine") patient was the inspiration for her debut novel, *Miracle Creek*. This courtroom thriller tackles themes of immigration, parenting, and autism.

One example of a hyperbaric oxygen therapy submarine!

Yangsze Choo's favorite childhood book was *My Family and Other Animals* by Gerald Durrell. Her love of his books about rare animals and zoo conservation is what influenced her to include many animals in *The Night Tiger*. Her first novel, *The Ghost Bride*, is a Netflix Original Series. (Reese's Book Club pick, April 2019)

INFLUENTIAL BOOK PEOPLE

Ballantine Books 2018 hardcover, design by Sharanya Durvasula, art by Alexandra Bowman

GLORY EDIM

Founder and CEO of Well-Read Black Girl
Instagram: @wellreadblackgirl

Well-Read Black Girl was founded by Glory Edim in 2015. It is a book-club-turned-literary-festival based in Brooklyn, NY.

"My mission is to provoke conversations around publishing and to amplify new work by Black artists, from authors to activists to playwrights to policymakers. I use literature and storytelling as a tool for advocacy; I want to empower young Black girls and women to define success on their own terms. Whether you're reading Zora Neale Hurston, Alice Walker, or Toni Morrison, you will encounter the words of powerful writers who never lost sight of their vision. Whenever I read their books—and I tend to reread often—I am inspired by their talent, rigor, and limitless imagination.

Each of these books can be read as a primer to understanding the vast and wonderfully complex identity that is Black girlhood and womanhood. I believe reading is one of the most important aspects of one's livelihood and education. It is the foundation for all other knowledge to be absorbed. My life has been transformed by literature. We will always need more books written by Black women—each narrative provides us with hope and adds to our rich legacy, and ultimately, the act of storytelling helps us survive. As Well-Read Black Girl evolves, we will always center the stories of Black women."

LUPITA AQUINO

Lupita Aquino is the book curator for BESE, the media company founded by actress and activist Zoe Saldana. She is also a columnist at the *Washington Independent Review of Books* and co-founder of LIT on H St Book Club.

Instagram: @lupita.reads

Twitter: @lupita_reads

"I spend a lot of time trying to reflect and put into words what books have done for me. How simply reading a story can propel so much emotion and internal healing for someone like me. The titles listed below have given me the language to identify who I am in the world, but most importantly, they have opened up channels of self-reflection I didn't know I needed at the time. In many ways that self-reflection has saved me. This self-reflection contributes to the way I show up in the world and in many cases reading this stack of books has given me the power to live authentically. Reading *So Far from God* by Ana Castillo in my teens literally showed me it was possible to exist as queer and Mexican while *The Namesake* by Jhumpa Lahiri gave me the ability to see what it might have been like for my immigrant parents navigating a world so different from their home country. Outside of self-reflections, these books have helped me forge connections with the community around me and push me to want to share my own stories with others."

BOOK CLUB DARLINGS

Oprah Winfrey revolutionized book clubs when she launched her own on her talk show in 1996. While readers still enjoy the traditional format of meeting in person to discuss the latest best sellers, social media and virtual platforms have made book clubs even more accessible to millions of readers around the world.

The favorite beverage of Sportcoat, the protagonist

When asked what he thinks readers can learn from *Deacon King Kong*, James McBride replied, "The aim of the book is to show people that we are all alike, that our aims are the same and that we are more alike than we are different. We're currently at a time where we need to be reminded about humanity and our heritage, and the fact that courage, modesty, and morality are still the spine that holds America together." (Oprah's Book Club pick, June 2020)

Houghton Mifflin Harcourt 2021 hardcover, art by Rupert Meats/Rude

Mateo Askaripour was director of sales development at a startup but quit his job in 2016 to become a writer. His debut novel *Black Buck* is a cautionary tale about losing yourself in such a career but also includes practical tips on how to succeed at it. While the book is a satire, Askaripour says it is "completely factual when it comes to my emotions. I have felt every single thing that these characters feel." (Read With Jenna pick, January 2021)

Following the success of her best-selling debut novel, *The Mothers*, Brit Bennett's highly anticipated second novel, *The Vanishing Half*, debuted at number one on the *New York Times* fiction best-seller list. Inspired by a story that her mother told her, this multigenerational family saga is slated to be adapted into an HBO limited series with Bennett executive producing. (*Good Morning America* Book Club pick, June 2020)

Riverhead Books 2020 hardcover, design and art by Lauren Peters-Collaer

Park Row 2020 hardcover

Nancy Jooyoun Kim knows firsthand how valuable independent bookstores are to communities. She worked at Elliott Bay Book Company in Seattle for a year, and she believes that "bookstores and libraries are the heart of a community and are vital to making our social spaces feel welcoming, intimate, alive, and engaged with the world." Her debut novel, *The Last Story of Mina Lee*, is a thrilling mystery exploring the relationship between an immigrant mother and her American-born daughter. (Reese's Book Club pick, September 2020)

Celeste Ng's best-selling novel *Little Fires Everywhere* premiered as a Hulu drama series featuring Kerry Washington and Reese Witherspoon in March 2020.

This was the Well-Read Black Girl Book Club pick for September 2019.
The story of Adunni, a 14-year-old Nigerian girl seeking to find her voice while fighting for her right to an education
The Belletrist Book Club March 2020 pick
The story of a henna artist in 1950s Jaipur striving for her independence
A Cherokee family mourns the loss of their teenage son, Ray-Ray, who was shot by a police officer 15 years before.
A wildly entertaining debut novel about Afi, who resists cultural norms and her family's expectations of an arranged marriage.
Amerie's Book Club pick for July 2020
This was Roxane Gay's Audacious Book Club pick for April 2021.
The story of a fractured Colombian family trying to find the American Dream
THE GIRL WITH THE LOUDING VOICE ABI DARÉ
EVERYTHING INSIDE EDWIDGE DANTICAT
ANGIE CRUZ DOMINICANA
Such a Fun Age KILEY REID
THESE GHOSTS ARE FAMILY MAISY CARD
THE REMOVED BRANDON HOBSON
TAYARI JONES AN AMERICAN MARRIAGE
ALKA JOSHI The HENNA ARTIST
his only wife peace adzo medie
You Exist Too Much ZAINA ARAFAT
NAIMA COSTER WHAT'S MINE AND YOURS
Black Buck Mateo Askaripour
the PROPOSAL JASMINE GUILLORY
Deacon King Kong James McBride
A WOMAN IS NO MAN ETAF RUM
THE VANISHING HALF BRIT BENNETT
A BURNING MEGHA MAJUMDAR
Behold the DREAMERS IMBOLO MBUE
WELCOME TO LAGOS Chibundu Onuzo
LAUREN WILKINSON AMERICAN SPY
NEXT YEAR in HAVANA CHANEL CLEETON
Celeste Ng Little Fires Everywhere
The Last Story of Mina Lee Nancy Jooyoun Kim
MILK BLOOD HEAT DANTIEL W. MONIZ
EROTIC STORIES FOR PUNJABI WIDOWS BALLI KAUR JASWAL
LUSTER Raven Leilani
little gods MENG JIN
PATSY NICOLE DENNIS-BENN
INFINITE COUNTRY PATRICIA ENGEL

AUTHORS RECOMMEND

BRIT BENNETT

Author of *The Vanishing Half* and *The Mothers*

Instagram/Twitter: @britrbennett

Putnam 2019 hardcover, design by Vi-An Nguyen

Such A Fun Age
by Kiley Reid

"I loved Kiley Reid's *Such a Fun Age*, a smart, propulsive, and funny novel about a Black babysitter navigating the complicated and cringeworthy good intentions of her white boss. Reid writes about the complexity of navigating the relationship between race and labor with precision and wit; this book made me uncomfortable in the best way, and I couldn't put it down."

ANGIE KIM

Author of *Miracle Creek*

Instagram: @angiekimask
Twitter: @AngieKimWriter

Ecco 2020 hardcover, design by Sara Wood, art by Jessica Brilli

Leave the World Behind
by Rumaan Alam

"I can't stop raving about this book! First, as a writer, I have to talk about how much I loved his prose. He uses such unusual words, chosen with obvious care, to efficiently express in one six-word sentence what might take me three long sentences to express. And as a reader, I love dystopian novels, and the premise blew me away. It was suspenseful and kept me turning the pages all night long—what the f&$k is going on in the world?!?!?!?!?—and although it doesn't have anything to do with the pandemic, it resonated so perfectly with the sense of confusion, doom, and isolation so many of us felt. I've been recommending it to everyone I know!"

YAMILE SAIED MÉNDEZ

Author of *Furia* and *Where Are You From?*

Instagram/Twitter: @yamilesmendez

Arthur A. Levine 2019 hardcover, design by Maeve Norton, art by Joe Cepeda

The Moon Within
by Aida Salazar

"This magical novel in verse tells the journey of a girl on the cusp of leaving childhood behind as she's about to get her first period. Navigating all the changes puberty brings physically, emotionally, and socially, Celi's also on a quest to ascertain her personality even if it means going against her mom's wishes of participating in an ancestral Mexica ritual, a moon ceremony. Not only for girls, this book is funny, sensitive, and poignant. I wish I had Celi's story when I was a young girl grappling with life's big questions. And I also wish I'd had a moon ceremony."

MITCHELL S. JACKSON

Author of *Survival Math: Notes on an All-American Family*

Instagram/Twitter: @mitchsjackson

Riverhead 2019 hardcover, design by Alex Merto

Lot: Stories
by Bryan Washington

"Three of my favorite books are short story collections: Denis Johnson's *Jesus' Son*, Edward P. Jones's *All Aunt Hagar's Children*, and Junot Díaz's *Drown*. Well, this year, I read Bryan Washington's *Lot*, and at once determined it a book that should be mentioned among those greats. I love Washington's exploration of his home city of Houston and its rich cultural milieu, the artistry with which he explores coming of age, sexuality, and the promise of the American dream. I came away feeling as though I was an interloper in the neighborhood, as if his characters were humans whose lives I was invested in. *Lot* is a book I'll revisit for years to come, a book for lovers of short stories, for anyone who appreciates phenomenal fiction."

MIRA JACOB

Author of *Good Talk* and *The Sleepwalker's Guide to Dancing*

Instagram: @goodtalkthanks
Twitter: @mirajacob

The God of Small Things
by Arundhati Roy

Random House 2008 paperback, design by Anna Bauer

"Arundhati Roy's *The God of Small Things* was the first novel I read that centered my own community, the Syrian Christians of Kerala. I was young when it came out and had only ever seen us novelized as sidekicks and conquests, so reading us as rendered by Roy—especially the contradiction of our socialist history and rigid class consciousness—felt like looking into a mirror. What a relief to have the pain we inflicted on ourselves and others called out, named, and reimagined. What a gift."

Mira Nair directed the 2006 film based on this novel, which starred Irrfan Khan, Tabu, Kal Penn, and Sahira Nair.

An epic story of three families covering four generations set in Zambia, Africa

A portrait of an Indian American Muslim family gathering for their daughter's wedding

Set in Chicago's South Side, this debut novel explores faith, family secrets and friendship.

Told by five narrators, Kim's debut novel centers family dynamics and a complex love triangle during the Korean War.

A thriller told from ten points of view, those of the women (and one man) of an extended Métis family

Two Brooklyn families brought together by the marriage of their high school-aged children who are expecting a child

A story about love and family, set in India just after independence

FAMILY SAGAS

We read about other families to better understand the dynamics of our own, to understand why we all behave the ways we do, especially when faced with events beyond our control. These are books you can sink into, submerse yourself in for days, and come out gasping, feeling you have lived a whole other life.

About *Pachinko*, the multigenerational story of a Korean family in Japan, Min Jin Lee wrote, "I'm interested in creating radical empathy through art." She feels that "[literature is] one of the few things that can really convince human beings to view each other as human beings," and that it is her job to tell a story well enough to change the reader into a more empathic person than they were before, one who can no longer dehumanize another group of people.

Pachinko is a mechanical arcade and gambling game popular in Japan.

Helen Oyeyemi often uses fairy tales as a jumping-off point for her novels, because they show "truths that we sometimes want to look away from." She then spins her own take on the tale, making it something fresh, demonstrating both its timelessness and timeliness. To examine issues of race and beauty in *Boy, Snow, Bird*, Oyeyemi uses Snow White, since Oyeyemi "found it so strange how she could be so mild and so sweet after everything she's gone through." As with many of her books, this one focuses on women—the three title words are the names of the three main female characters. When asked about it, she said, "I just want to find out about all the different lives a woman can live. But my feminism has never been against men. It's not erasure; it's just they're not the focus."

Riverhead Books 2014 hardcover, design by Helen Yentus

As a young boy, Noa, the protagonist of *Sharks in the Time of Saviors*, is saved from drowning by a shiver of sharks. When asked about his inspiration, Kawai Strong Washburn said, "An image just spontaneously appeared in my head: a child in the water, gently carried to the surface by sharks. I have no idea where it came from." He contemplated it for years before eventually connecting it to his feelings about growing up in Hawai'i and writing this novel. Imbolo Mbue, reviewing it for the *New York Times*, writes that Washburn wants us "to see Hawai'i in its totality: as a place of proud ancestors and gods and spirits, but also of crumbling families and hopelessness and poverty. Of mystery and beauty at every corner."

LITTLE FREE DIVERSE LIBRARIES

Sarah Kamya grew up in a mainly white town in Massachusetts, and as a young, avid reader, she wished for more books about children like herself. Kamya is now an elementary school counselor in Manhattan, but in 2020, back in her hometown during the Covid-19 pandemic shutdown, she realized there was a simple thing she could do. She filled her local Little Free Library with children's books full of Black and brown main characters, thereby creating the first Little Free Diverse Library.

She then created @LittleFreeDiverseLibraries on Instagram, initially hoping for donations to fill just the LFLs in her town, but her brilliant idea took off, and book donations began streaming in (especially after an appearance on *The Today Show*!). She has since sent curated sets of books to hundreds of libraries all over the country and inspired countless other people to turn their own local LFLs into LFDLs.

"I believe that books have the power to start conversations and create change," Kamya says.

"I believe that Black and brown children deserve to see themselves represented in books," and "I am also excited for white children to educate themselves and experience different cultures and backgrounds through Black characters."

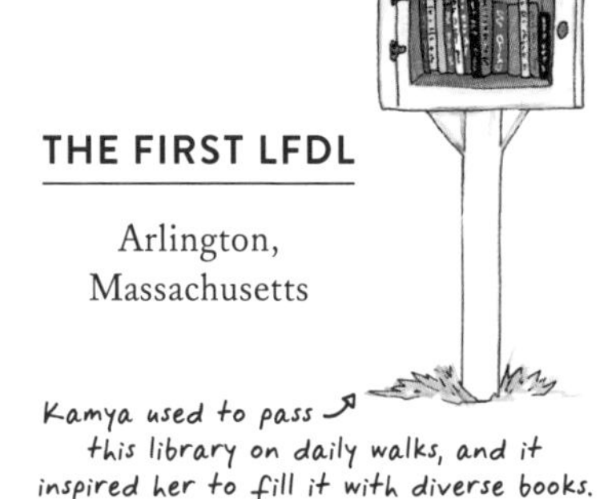

THE FIRST LFDL

Arlington, Massachusetts

Kamya used to pass this library on daily walks, and it inspired her to fill it with diverse books.

Want to turn your local LFL into an LFDL? Here are twelve books for kids and adults that Kamya recommends to get started! (But there are so many more out there, don't feel limited!)

@littlefreediversedallas is on a mission to fill all the LFLs in Dallas, and this was the 100th!

FIRE STATION LIBRARY

Dallas, Texas

F.R.E.E. LIBRARY

Lakeville, Minnesota

@f.r.e.e.library

PRINCESS GARDENS LIBRARY

Toronto, Ontario, Canada

Yes, there are many in Canada too! Check out @littlefreediverselibrariescan.

LITTLE DIVERSE LIBRARY

Madison, New Jersey

Girl Scouts Libby and Charlotte Nebres built and installed this LFDL at the Museum of Early Trades & Crafts!

ONE LOVE, ONE WORLD, MANY STORIES LIBRARY

Lowell, Massachusetts

How adorable is this @littlefreediverselowelllibrary?

LITTLE FREE ANTI-RACIST LIBRARY

Charlotte, North Carolina

@littlefreeantiracistlibrary

DIVERSE LITTLE FREE LIBRARY

Norridge, Illinois

This @littlefreediversenorridge library is always packed with books!

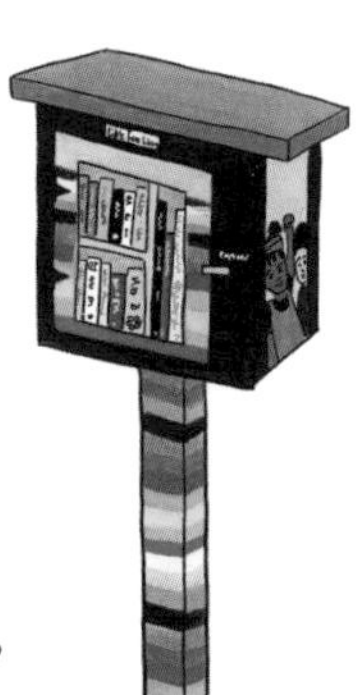

EMPOWER LIBRARY

West Roxbury, Massachusetts

See more LFDLs in the area @wrdiverselibraries.

BOOKISH PEOPLE RECOMMEND

Grand Central 2020 paperback

CREE MYLES

Curator of All Ways Black

Instagram: @creemyles

Wild Seed
by Octavia E. Butler

"Octavia Butler was a god among (white) men and while everything that she created flipped the science fiction genre on its head, *Wild Seed* is her most magnificent creation. Two shape-shifting demigods who have to learn to coexist or perish while confronting the transatlantic slave trade eventually leading them to the antebellum south. It is brilliant."

CHRISTINE BOLLOW

Programs and marketing manager at Loyalty Bookstores

Instagram: @readingismagical

Viking 2018 hardcover, design by Matt Vee

America is Not the Heart
by Elaine Castillo

"This is a quiet yet powerful, character-driven story that follows Hero, a Filipina immigrant building a new life in America. I ask you to read this because I want my people, my culture, my family to be seen. Filipinx representation in the media has been terribly underrepresented and our stories deserve to be heard."

Milkweed Editions 2021 paperback, art by Holly Young

SASHA MARIA S.

Ojibwe bookstagrammer

Instagram: @anishinaabekwereads

The Seed Keeper
by Diane Wilson

"Diane Wilson (Dakhóta) is a stunning writer and her character-driven fiction debut is a work of art. *The Seed Keeper* is a stunning exploration of how a shared past, both Indigenous and non-Indigenous, structures our present and future. Following Rosalie Iron Wing, we see the complexities of Dakhóta identity, life, loss, and homecoming on individual and communal levels. This book resonated deeply, making me reflect on Indigenous knowledge about history, plants, and lands and how these knowledges help us come back home after dislocation and disconnection. A beautifully written emotional and reflective story that keeps you going until the last page."

DONNA JOHNSON

Founder and curator of This BrowneGirl Reads Reading Community

Instagram: @thisbrownegirlreads

Song of Solomon
by Toni Morrison

Knopf 1977 hardcover, design by R. D. Scudellari

"*Song of Solomon* is my favorite Morrison. I think that if one is going to select only one of her works, this has to be it. The novel, which was Morrison's third, reveals the master storyteller we've come to love. There aren't many narratives that can keep you captured with its many characters while holding them to their individual contributions to the tale. In this coming-of-age story, Toni writes with brilliance a story for the ages, one that is still discussed 43 years after it was written."

Scribner 2018 hardcover, design by Na Kim

MORGAN HARDING

Bookseller, Politics and Prose Bookstore

Instagram: @morgan__gayle

Heavy
by Kiese Laymon

"This is one of the best books I've ever read. He has his own unique writing voice which makes him one of the best American writers alive. Written in the second person, Laymon writes to his mother about growing up as a young Black man in Mississippi under her care. Despite his struggles as a child, it is clear that Laymon loves his family, Blackness, and Black people."

CRYSTAL FORTE

Author/Educational specialist

Instagram: @melanatedreader

The Secret Lives of Church Ladies
by Deesha Philyaw

West Virginia University Press 2020 paperback, design by Stewart Williams, photo by Sewn Apart

"Have you ever read a collection of short stories that consumed you, leaving you completely thrown into the minds of individuals in a way that sticks with you for weeks after you've read the story? Deesha Philyaw's *The Secret Lives of Church Ladies* does just that. As I progressed through each story, the stories got better and better. As a reader, you are left wondering how this is possible. Although you want to separate them and rank your favorite, it is impossible to not think of this collection as a whole. Each story carries its own message that intertwines faith and contemporary folklore with seeping wisdom at its core."

HISTORICAL FICTION

A historical novel is the next best thing to a time machine—there is always something new to learn when you pick one up. When reading these deeply woven stories you can gain new insight on historical events and discover untold stories and people you never knew about along the way. Historical fiction creates a fine journey to the past while shining the light on the present.

Akashic 2016 hardcover, design by Jason Harvey

Winner of the 2017 NAACP Image Award for Outstanding Literary Work in Fiction, *The Book of Harlan* journeys through monumental historical events like the Great Migration, the Harlem Renaissance, the Holocaust, and the Civil Rights era. McFadden's family history is woven into the story, and Harlan is based on her grandfather, who is featured on the cover. McFadden has also written erotica under the pseudonym Geneva Holliday.

Kaitlyn Greenidge's second novel, *Libertie*, is inspired by the life of one of the first Black female doctors in the United States. Her debut novel, *We Love You, Charlie Freeman,* won the 2017 Whiting Award for Fiction.

Algonquin Books 2021 hardcover, design by Christopher Moisan, art by Laurindo Feliciano

Atria Books 2020 hardcover, design by Donna Cheng

Susan Abulhawa is the founder of Playgrounds for Palestine, an organization dedicated to upholding Palestinian children's right to play, even under occupation and in refugee camps abroad. *Against the Loveless World* centers on the story of Nahr, a Palestinian woman reflecting on her life while in solitary confinement in an Israeli prison. Abulhawa's debut novel, *Mornings in Jenin,* was an international best seller and has been translated into 30 languages.

Susan Abulhawa published a poetry collection titled "My Voice Sought the Wind" in 2013.

Yaa Gyasi's stunning debut novel is a sweeping generational story about two sisters in Ghana—Effia, who is married to a white slave trader and lives in a castle in Cape Coast, and Esi, who is captured and placed in the atrocious dungeon of the castle where her sister resides and is eventually shipped to America in the cross-Atlantic slave trade. Gyasi was the recipient of the National Book Foundation's 2016 5 Under 35 prize, awarded to debut fiction writers.

Knopf 2016 hardcover, design by Peter Mendelsund

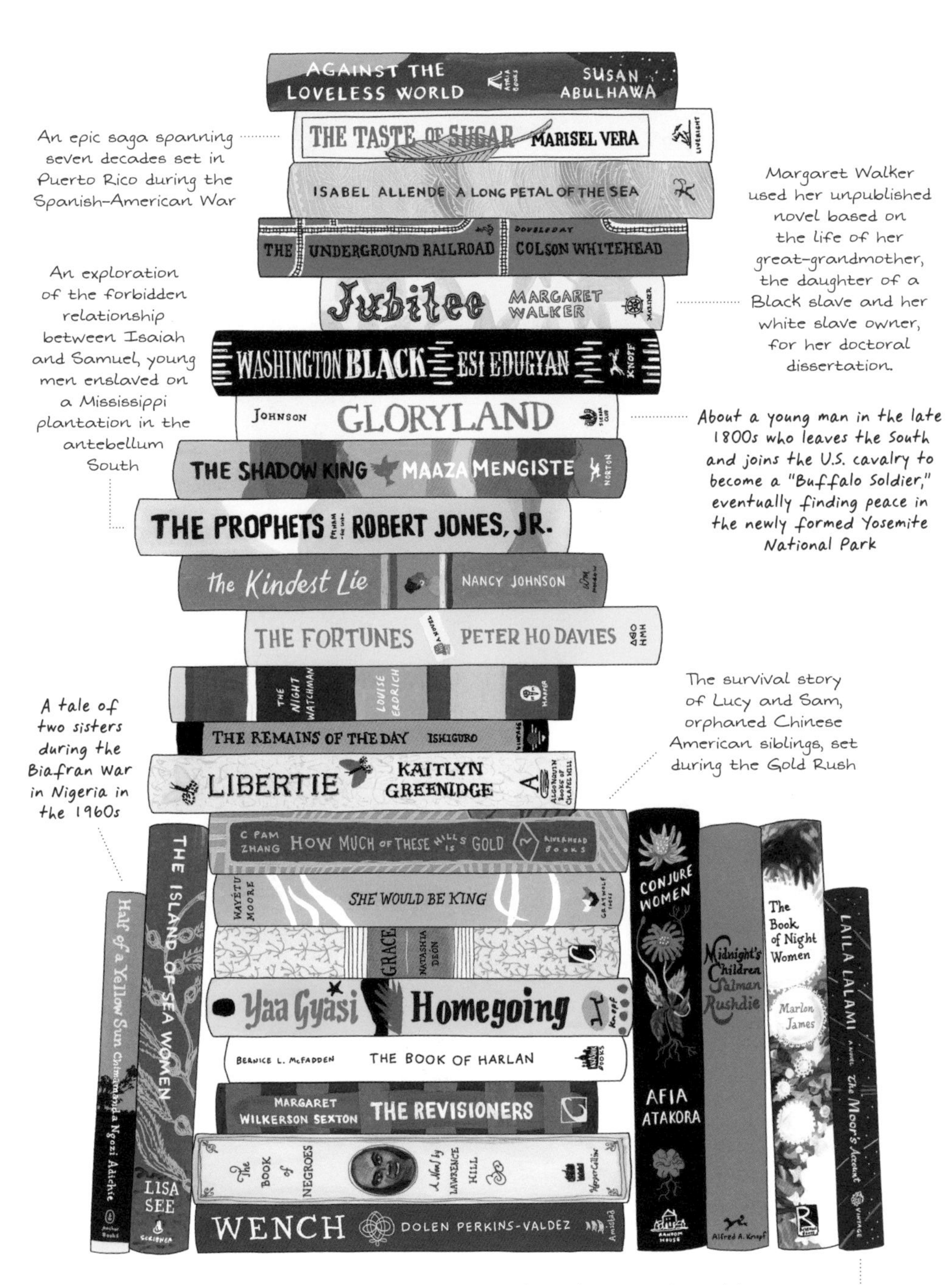

AGAINST THE LOVELESS WORLD
SUSAN ABULHAWA
ATRIA BOOKS
An epic saga spanning seven decades set in Puerto Rico during the Spanish-American War
THE TASTE OF SUGAR
MARISEL VERA
LIVERIGHT
ISABEL ALLENDE
A LONG PETAL OF THE SEA
Margaret Walker used her unpublished novel based on the life of her great-grandmother, the daughter of a Black slave and her white slave owner, for her doctoral dissertation.
THE UNDERGROUND RAILROAD
DOUBLEDAY
COLSON WHITEHEAD
An exploration of the forbidden relationship between Isaiah and Samuel, young men enslaved on a Mississippi plantation in the antebellum South
Jubilee
MARGARET WALKER
MARINER
WASHINGTON BLACK
ESI EDUGYAN
KNOPF
JOHNSON
GLORYLAND
About a young man in the late 1800s who leaves the South and joins the U.S. cavalry to become a "Buffalo Soldier," eventually finding peace in the newly formed Yosemite National Park
THE SHADOW KING
MAAZA MENGISTE
NORTON
THE PROPHETS
ROBERT JONES, JR.
the Kindest Lie
NANCY JOHNSON
THE FORTUNES
A NOVEL
PETER HO DAVIES
HMH
THE NIGHT WATCHMAN
LOUISE ERDRICH
HARPER
The survival story of Lucy and Sam, orphaned Chinese American siblings, set during the Gold Rush
A tale of two sisters during the Biafran War in Nigeria in the 1960s
THE REMAINS OF THE DAY
ISHIGURO
VINTAGE
LIBERTIE
KAITLYN GREENIDGE
ALGONQUIN BOOKS OF CHAPEL HILL
C PAM ZHANG
HOW MUCH OF THESE HILLS IS GOLD
RIVERHEAD BOOKS
WAYÉTU MOORE
SHE WOULD BE KING
GRAYWOLF PRESS
GRACE
NATASHIA DEON
Yaa Gyasi
Homegoing
Knopf
BERNICE L. McFADDEN
THE BOOK OF HARLAN
MARGARET WILKERSON SEXTON
THE REVISIONERS
The BOOK of NEGROES
A Novel by LAWRENCE HILL
HarperCollins
WENCH
DOLEN PERKINS-VALDEZ
Amistad
Half of a Yellow Sun
Chimamanda Ngozi Adichie
Anchor Books
THE ISLAND OF SEA WOMEN
LISA SEE
SCRIBNER
CONJURE WOMEN
AFIA ATAKORA
RANDOM HOUSE
Midnight's Children
Salman Rushdie
Alfred A. Knopf
The Book of Night Women
Marlon James
LAILA LALAMI
A NOVEL
The Moor's Account
VINTAGE
Laila Lalami imagines the memoirs of Mustafa al-Zamori, a.k.a. Estebanico, who was the slave of a Spanish conquistador and became an explorer himself.

LEGENDS

OCTAVIA E. BUTLER

(1947–2006)

Dawn

Grand Central Publishing 2021 paperback, design and art by Jim Tierney

Dawn is the first book in the Xenogenesis trilogy. This dystopian novel begins with an uninhabitable Earth after a nuclear war, and the remaining survivors find themselves rescued by an alien spacecraft.

Penguin Books 2006 paperback, design by Elizabeth Yaffe, art by Kathy Kim

AMY TAN

(1952–)

The Joy Luck Club

Tan's debut novel about the relationship between Chinese immigrant mothers and their American-born daughters incorporates her family experiences and has resonated with readers for more than 30 years.

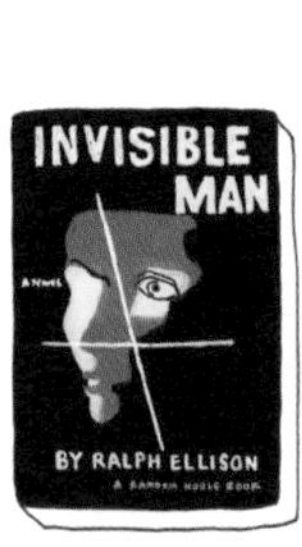

Random House 1952 hardcover, design by Edward McKnight Kauffer

RALPH ELLISON

(1914–1994)

Invisible Man

Ellison wrote *Invisible Man* while he was on leave from the merchant marines. It took him five years to complete his first novel, which won the National Book Award for Fiction in 1953.

AUDRE LORDE

(1934–1992)

Zami: A New Spelling of My Name

Crossing Press 2020 paperback, design by Lizzie Allen, art by Alexis Eke

Lorde explores her identity as Black, female, and lesbian in what she coined a "biomythography," which combines history, biography, and myth-making.

ALICE WALKER

(1944–)

The Color Purple

Celie's story of survival despite the horrors in her life won Walker the 1983 Pulitzer Prize for Fiction and the National Book Award for Fiction. This modern classic was also adapted into a film and a musical.

Harcourt Brace Jovanovich 1982 hardcover, design by Judith Kazdym Leeds

Bantam 1973 paperback

MAYA ANGELOU

(1928–2014)

Just Give Me a Cool Drink of Water 'Fore I Diiie

Nominated for the Pulitzer Prize, Angelou's first book of poetry features 38 poems exploring love, race, class, politics, poverty, and addiction.

Penguin Essentials 2016 paperback art by Laurent Moreau

GABRIEL GARCÍA MÁRQUEZ

(1927–2014)

Love in the Time of Cholera

This timeless love triangle story spanning more than 50 years was first published in Spanish in 1985. García Márquez's beloved novel was also adapted into a movie.

RICHARD WRIGHT

(1908–1960)

Black Boy

Harper Perennial 2008 paperback

Wright, the descendant of slaves and the son of a sharecropper, details his turbulent experiences growing up in the Jim Crow South in his 1945 memoir.

Stories of Your Life and Others TED CHIANG
SOUR HEART JENNY ZHANG
Drinking Coffee Elsewhere ZZ PACKER
IF I HAD TWO WINGS RANDALL KENAN NORTON
LAND OF BIG NUMBERS TE-PING CHEN
THINGS WE LOST IN THE FIRE MARIANA ENRIQUEZ HOGARTH
MACHADO HER BODY AND OTHER PARTIES
ADJEI-BRENYAH FRIDAY BLACK
DUNNING ANNIE MUKTUK and OTHER STORIES
THIS ACCIDENT OF BEING LOST LEANNE BETASAMOSAKE SIMPSON
SABRINA & CORINA KALI FAJARDO-ANSTINE ONE WORLD
HOW TO PRONOUNCE KNIFE SOUVANKHAM THAMMAVONGSA
THE SECRET LIVES OF CHURCH LADIES PHILYAW
EVERYDAY PEOPLE JENNIFER BAKER, EDITOR
ZALIKA REID-BENTA FRYING PLANTAIN ASTORIA
THE AWKWARD BLACK MAN WALTER MOSLEY
This Is Paradise Kristiana Kahakauwila Hogarth
LOVE WAR STORIES IVELISSE RODRIGUEZ
HOW TO LOVE A JAMAICAN ALEXIA ARTHURS
LOT BRYAN WASHINGTON Riverhead Books
Jhumpa Lahiri Interpreter of Maladies
NETTEL BEZOAR and Other Unsettling Stories
IN THE COUNTRY MIA ALVAR
Gorilla, My Love
Short Stories by Toni Cade Bambara
RANDOM HOUSE
HEADS OF THE COLORED PEOPLE NAFISSA THOMPSON-SPIRES
EDITED BY PATRICE CALDWELL A PHOENIX FIRST MUST BURN VIKING
XUAN JULIANA WANG HOME REMEDIES Hogarth
THE WORLD DOESN'T REQUIRE YOU RION AMILCAR SCOTT
THE KING IS ALWAYS ABOVE THE PEOPLE DANIEL ALARCÓN Riverhead Books
SORRY PLEASE THANK YOU CHARLES YU
SHRUTI SWAMY A HOUSE IS A BODY
THE OFFICE OF HISTORICAL CORRECTIONS DANIELLE EVANS RIVERHEAD BOOKS
A debut short story collection examining modern-day China and its diaspora
Stories narrated by the daughters of Chinese immigrants living in New York
Brilliant satirical stories on racism and consumer culture
This won Canada's Danuta Gleed Literary Award in 2018.
A collection of stories set mostly in the workplace capturing the everyday lives of refugees and immigrants
Interconnected stories about a girl growing up in the Little Jamaica neighborhood of Toronto
Short stories from the author of the award-winning "Interior Chinatown"

STORY COLLECTIONS

Short stories are intense, delightful nuggets of fiction. When it's inexplicably hard to hold focus for long, novels can seem daunting, but a short story feels just right. You will still be transported and distracted, but briefly enough that the world won't be able to fall apart in the meantime.

Randall Kenan's 1989 novel, *A Visitation of Spirits*, his 1992 collection of stories, *Let the Dead Bury Their Dead*, and his 2020 collection, *If I Had Two Wings*, are all set in the fictional rural town of Tims Creek, North Carolina. Kenan's work has often been called magical realism, and while he found the term "reductive," he did love the "Latin boom" of writers like García Márquez, Fuentes, and Allende. He said, "What I got from them was permission to look at the world with the eyes that I'd grown up with, as opposed to the rigid social realism that has dominated Southern literature for all of the twentieth century."

Kenan died at age 57 in August of 2020, barely a month after the release of "If I Had Two Wings."

Norton 2020 hardcover, design by Yang Kim

Kristiana Kahakauwila describes herself as "a hapa writer of kanaka maoli (Native Hawaiian), German, and Norwegian descent." She grew up in California, and when visiting her family on Maui, she could see the stark differences between the mainland tourist version of Hawai'i and the islands where locals live their everyday lives. About *This Is Paradise* she says, "I'm undermining the idea of the scrubbed-up Disneyland of Waikiki and, in the stories that follow that first one, I believe I'm offering Hawai'i as complex, [and] beautiful in that complexity."

Nafissa Thompson-Spires grew up in Southern California reading "voraciously" as a child, and says, "I had more book friends than human friends. I was really into Judy Blume. And I loved Sweet Valley Twins and the Baby-Sitters Club." When asked by the *Guardian* what motivated her to write *Heads of the Colored People*, she said, "I wanted to see more stories about awkward, nerdy Black people, and Black people who were the only ones in a particular space, and what it meant to navigate the many different kinds of identity construct. You write what you want to read. You're reshaping an ongoing conversation."

37 Ink 2019 paperback, design by Emma A. Van Deun, art by Rodrigo Corral Design, Inc.

WRITING ROOMS

One World 2019 hardcover design by Sharanya Durvasula, art by Gustavo Rimada

KALI FAJARDO-ANSTINE

Author of *Sabrina & Corina: Stories*
Instagram: @kalimaja / Twitter: @KaliMaFaja

"I live in a loft apartment in downtown Denver in a building from 1910. The layout is a long oblong shape, and the large windows are filled with bright light. The space is inspiring because of the history within the stone building (I'm almost certain it houses many ghosts). I have artwork from Colorado artist Daniel Luna and different artifacts from my writing research and travels—there's a coal miner's lantern, rocks and pottery from the Southwest, and an Our Lady of Guadalupe candle atop my writing desk. My godmother gave me this green lamp, and I love how it shines its hue across the desk."

Ecco 2018 hardcover, design by Allison Saltzman

RUMAAN ALAM

Author of *Leave the World Behind* and *That Kind of Mother*
Instagram: @rumaanalam / Twitter: @Rumaan

"This is the interior room on the top floor of a small house—so no window, but a skylight. My desk is in the corner. It is campaign-sized, and the chair is a beat-up old dining chair with this amazing fabric on it (we've a loveseat in the same fabric, which I often use as a backdrop for book photos on Instagram). The painting on the desk was by me at age 14, the sculpture is by Kehinde Wiley, and it's sitting in a Lucite tray full of rubbish. The pile of books is almost always on the top unless I lose my mind and throw them all over the floor. There's a yellow chair along the wall to my right when I sit, and there's a pile of books on it for an essay I was supposed to write and never did, yikes. Over the desk—the painting of the Black woman holding a phone is by Jas Knight, there's a drawing by a childhood friend, a painting of a whale done by my older son when he was four, and the painting on the pink backdrop is so cool, I don't know why I can't recall the artist's name. There's a 50-franc bill (has the Little Prince on it!) tucked into the frame.

The wall to the right has more art—you can see an old mirror with photos tucked into it and a drawing of two kids over top, but there's more. The closet doorknob always has tote bags on it. The plug situation underfoot is out of control."

BOOKISH PEOPLE RECOMMEND

Knopf 1973 hardcover, design by Wendell Minor

KIMBERLY V. NELSON

Writer

Instagram: @missberlyreads

Sula
by Toni Morrison

"*Sula* is a favorite I reread annually. I'm captivated by Morrison's lyrical and efficient prose. While the story is about the ups and downs of the lifelong friendship between Nel and Sula, it's memorable in how it examines what freedom means to generations of Black women in their families."

Granta 2017 paperback, art by Sinem Erkas

NOKUKHANYA NTSALUBA

Travel writer and bookstagrammer

Instagram: @pretty_x_bookish

Under the Udala Trees
by Chinelo Okparanta

"Whoever said there were no beautiful queer stories coming out of Africa clearly hadn't read this stunningly tender portrayal of queer love, friendship, family, womanhood, and what it means to find one's self in love. This book will break your heart and stitch it back together."

SACHI ARGABRIGHT

Bookstagrammer

Instagram: @sachireads

Pachinko
by Min Jin Lee

Grand Central Publishing 2017 hardcover

"*Pachinko* impacted me so much as an Asian American reader, and it is a book I constantly recommend to others. As a half-Japanese woman, I believe it's important I understand Japan's role in colonization. *Pachinko* helped me better understand that, while also sweeping me into a beautiful multigenerational family saga."

ANABEL JIMENEZ

Bookstagrammer and publishing industry professional

Instagram: @inthebookcorner

Infinite Country
by Patricia Engel

Avid Reader Press 2021 hardcover, design by Grace Han

"One of the most honest and accurate portrayals of the immigrant experience in the United States that I have ever read. While reading, I saw my family's origin story reflected in these pages in a way I have never seen before. Though it's less than 200 pages, Engel's work packs a punch. Read this if you come from an immigrant background. Read this if you want a glimpse into our struggles, into our love, into our lives."

Ballantine Books 2018 hardcover, design and art by Caroline Teagle Johnson

CINDY ALLMAN

Founder of Read Caribbean (#readcaribbean)

Instagram/Twitter: @bookofcinz

How to Love a Jamaican
by Alexia Arthurs

"This is a book I will always recommend; it is a collection of short stories that perfectly captures the Jamaican experience. It is not every day you open a book and see yourself, family, and friends on the pages. This book is perfect for someone who is just getting back into reading—it covers universal themes such as love, identity, migration, family, and grief. The stories are so unique, the characters are layered, and it is a book that will get under your skin and stay there."

PARIS CLOSE

Founding editor of *Paperback Paris*

Instagram: @parisperusing

Real Life
by Brandon Taylor

Riverhead Books 2020 hardcover, design by Grace Han

"The best stories don't warn you that they will break your heart. Brandon Taylor does just that in his beautifully nuanced, painfully honest debut novel, *Real Life*. Spanning a single weekend, a gay Black graduate student named Wallace must overcome the unseeable hurdles of systemic racism, endless microaggressions within his all-white friend group, and the recoils of an unexpected interracial love affair. Like so many queer Black men, Wallace often feels unseen, unheard, and unmoored in the expanse of whiteness—wanting nothing more than a place, or a person, to call home. As a queer Black man, I was both relieved and rescued by *Real Life*, and it brings me the greatest joy to know a story like this finally exists for the next generation and beyond."

Milkweed Editions 2020 hardcover, art by Tony Drehfal

VICTORIA CASWELL

Bookstagrammer and teacher

Instagram: @floury_words

Braiding Sweetgrass: Indigenous Wisdom, Scientific Knowledge, and the Teachings of Plants
by Robin Wall Kimmerer

"In *Braiding Sweetgrass*, Robin Wall Kimmerer poetically writes about plants and animals while stating the importance of our relationship with land and place. Through the rich narrative, she intertwines oral tradition, myths, and Indigenous knowledge, while emphasizing that plants are our best teachers. All aspects of nature—plants, animals, humans, and land—are deeply intertwined. As Kimmerer says, 'We restore the land and the land restores us.' "

SPECULATIVE FICTION: OUR WORLD

All of these books take place here on Earth, the writers each using our reality as their starting point but then riffing on it, showing us other possible versions of it. The fact that our current sensory organs can't perceive those alternate realities doesn't mean they aren't out there.

N. K. Jemisin views her novel *The City We Became*, the first in a trilogy about New York City coming to life, as "an acknowledgement of all the complexity—the good, bad, ugly, and beautiful—that happens when you have so many people in a small space." In it, New York becomes a city great enough to be fully alive and earn human avatars, an apt person to represent each borough and one for the city overall. For the city to survive and thrive, the avatars must come together to fight a common enemy: a viral, gentrifying, homogenizing force of evil. On why it takes a team from many backgrounds, Jemisin compares it to *The Lord of the Rings*, and says, "You're not going to save the world with technology . . . You're going to save it with people choosing to fight against things that they perceive as wrong. In that sense, I'm a very traditional fantasy writer."

Orbit 2020 hardcover, design by Lauren Panepinto

Empire of Wild is a rich, dark story about deep, true love and the grief that can come with it, and also about a rogarou, a werewolf-like creature. Cherie Dimaline is a member of the Georgian Bay Métis community in Ontario, and when asked about young authors said, "The advice that I would give to emerging writers—especially from Black, Indigenous, and other people of color communities—is stay true to your voice. We desperately need your voice. We desperately need your stories."

The word "rogarou" (also spelled rougarou) comes from the French term for a werewolf: loup-garou.

In *Elatsoe*, Darcie Little Badger tells the story of Ellie, a 17-year-old asexual Lipan Apache woman who, like her family and ancestors, can call and train animal spirits. With the help of the ghost of her childhood springer spaniel, she sets out to solve the murder of her cousin. Little Badger made Ellie very human and relatable as a "tough, nerdy character who enjoys comic books," but also very specifically Native. "This is a Lipan book and not a Mescalero book because we are not a monolith. There's so many variations among cultures, the hundreds of tribal nations that are indigenous to this land."

A community turns to Anishinaabe traditions in the aftermath of an apocalypse.
Thirteen-year-old Amari Peters gets invited to a supernatural summer camp and hunts for her missing older brother.
A classic, published in 1975
About a school for Argentinian werewolves and witches!
A near-future thriller about sentience. Divya has degrees in computational neuroscience and signal processing and worked as an electrical engineer for 20 years.
A young woman takes a road trip with the Mayan god of death in 1920s Mexico.
More stunning stories from the author of "Stories of Your Life and Others"
EDEN ROBINSON SON OF A TRICKSTER
NALO HOPKINSON BROWN GIRL IN THE RING
WAUBGESHIG RICE MOON of the CRUSTED SNOW
ALSTON AMARI AND THE NIGHT BROTHERS
dhalgren samuel r. delany
THE PREY OF GODS NICKY DRAYDEN
RING SHOUT P. DJÈLI CLARK
LABYRINTH LOST ZORAIDA CÓRDOVA
LOBIZONA ROMINA GARBER
MACHINEHOOD S.B. DIVYA
THOMAS CEMETERY BOYS
COLSON WHITEHEAD THE INTUITIONIST
THE CITY WE BECAME N.K. JEMISIN
Nnedi Okorafor WHO FEARS DEATH
Solomon AN UNKINDNESS of GHOSTS
GODS OF JADE AND SHADOW SILVIA MORENO-GARCIA
NISI SHAWL EVERFAIR
EMPIRE OF WILD A NOVEL CHERIE DIMALINE
SIA MARTINEZ AND THE MOONLIT BEGINNING OF EVERYTHING GILLILAND
McKINNEY A BLADE SO BLACK
RIOT BABY TOCHI ONYEBUCHI
THE THREE-BODY PROBLEM CIXIN LIU
DEONN LEGENDBORN
AMERICAN WAR OMAR EL AKKAD
Parable of the Sower OCTAVIA E. BUTLER
ROSEWATER TADE THOMPSON
EXHALATION TED CHIANG
Little Badger Elatsoe
This debut novel is set in 2074, when a second American Civil War between the North and South breaks out.

BEAUTIFUL COVERS BY BRILLIANT DESIGNERS

Can you really say you've never judged a book by its cover? Well, there's an entire wonderful profession dedicated to getting you to do so. Here are some truly compelling book covers, created by designers from different backgrounds.

Vintage
2020 paperback

WOW, NO THANK YOU

by Samantha Irby

design by Joan Wong

Instagram: @jningwong

Wong prefers book cover design over other forms of design because "you're helping to sell something, but you're selling ideas, and narrative, and literacy."

Flatiron Books
2019 hardcover

THE NIGHT TIGER

by Yangsze Choo

design by
Mumtaz Mustafa

Instagram:
@mumtazmustafadesigns

Mustafa, a senior art director at HarperCollins, also designed the gorgeous covers of *Little Gods* by Meng Jin and *The Mountains Sing* by Nguyễn Phan Quế Mai.

Farrar, Strau, and
Giroux 2018 hardcover

SEVERANCE

by Ling Ma

design by Na Kim

Instagram: @na_son

When asked how she defines a successful cover, Kim said, "Success is when everyone's happy: the editor, the publisher, the author. We're designing books a year ahead of when they're released, so if I can still be really happy with the book when it comes out? Then I've done a good job."

Flatiron Books
2019 hardcover

DOMINICANA

by Angie Cruz

design by
Adalis Martinez

About this cover, Martinez posted to Instagram, "As a Dominicana, I've never felt more represented on anything I've ever worked on. The Dominican Republic is a tiny island in the Caribbean filled with so many stories." Martinez died of cancer in 2020, at just age 29.

Catapult
2020 hardcover

TO KEEP THE SUN ALIVE

by Rabeah Ghaffari

design by
Donna Cheng

Cheng, a senior designer at Simon & Schuster, also designed the covers for *Queenie* by Candice Carty-Williams and *The Book of Memory* by Petina Gappah.

Riverhead Books
2021 hardcover

MY YEAR ABROAD

by Chang-rae Lee

design by Grace Han

Instagram: @heaeunhan

Grace Han is an associate art director at Riverhead Books. On the future of book design, she says, "Books will need to be a covetable item while still being able to stand out as a thumbnail in the digital world." Han also designed the cover of *Real Life* by Brandon Taylor.

Tordotcom
2020 hardcover

RING SHOUT

by P. Djèlí Clark

design by
Henry Sene Yee

Instagram:
@henryseneyee_design

Yee has been designing book covers for over 30 years, falling into it by accident when record album cover design virtually quit being a thing. He also designed the cover of the memoir *Sigh, Gone* by Phuc Tran.

BLACK GIRL, CALL HOME

by Jasmine Mans

design by
Dominique Jones,
photo by
Micaiah Carter

Berkley 2021
paperback

Instagram:
@iamdominiqueee
@micaiahcarter

Jones is the founder of Black and Brown Book Designers (blackbookdesigners.com and @bnbbookdesigners on Instagram) "showcasing Black and Brown designers within the publishing industry."

Vintage 2018
paperback

STAY WITH ME

by Ayọ̀bámi Adébáyọ̀

design by
Linda Huang

Instagram:
@spiritditty

On book design, Huang says, "A book cover designer . . . distills the essence of a book to attract potential readers, or to put it simply, to advertise the book. It's a marketing tool as well as a type of visual literary criticism . . . Increasingly, I think it means giving the potential reader a sense of what it feels like to read the book."

BELOVED BOOKSTORES

The mural is by Sentrock!

SEMICOLON BOOKSTORE & GALLERY

Chicago, Illinois, USA
Instagram: @semicolonchi

After putting her dream of opening a luxurious membership club, library, and coworking space on hold, Danielle Mullen stumbled across vacant retail space while taking a leisurely walk. With no idea what she would use the space for, she began to fill the location with the things that she loved. This space would become what is now known as Semicolon Bookstore, the sole Black female–owned bookstore in Chicago. The bookstore-gallery was created to be comfortable and inviting, filled with books and art. Mullen holds a PhD in literary theory and has experience writing exhibition copy for art museums. When asked why the name "Semicolon," she said, "I love the idea of a sentence's ability to continue forward whenever the author so chooses. It's so applicable to other aspects of life, which is what I thought made it perfect for the space I was creating."

PALABRAS BILINGUAL BOOKSTORE

Phoenix, Arizona, USA
Instagram: @palabras_bookstore

Palabras Bilingual Bookstore, founded by Rosaura "Chawa" Magaña, is the only bilingual bookstore in Arizona. Magaña originally opened Palabras as an event space in 2015. By 2016, she had acquired enough books to officially launch the bookstore. Palabras promotes cultural representation, equity, and liberation through community engagement involving literature, language, and the arts. Palabras offers the Phoenix community books in Spanish and English, as well as zines, artisan wares, clothing, and works by local artists. Magaña believes in fostering an environment for intercultural community exchange, providing the community with opportunities to share literary, visual, and musical art through workshops and events.

MASSY BOOKS

Vancouver, British Columbia, Canada
Instagram: @massybooks

Massy Books is a champion of Indigenous authors and diversity. The store is 100% Indigenous owned and operated and a member of the Stó:lō Business Association. Owner Patricia Massy, who is Cree and English, comes from seven generations of booksellers, including Stephen Massey, founder of Christie's Auction House book department in New York. The 1,500-square-foot two-story space houses floor-to-ceiling shelves of science fiction, paperbacks, vintage comics, literary fiction, and a rare book collection. You can also find shelves dedicated to books by and about First Nations and Indigenous people. While browsing for books, don't forget to visit the 400-square-foot art gallery showcasing emerging artists in the community.

Neon Yang's Tensorate series is often described as "silkpunk," which author Ken Liu (who coined the term) defines as "a blend of science fiction and fantasy... [that] draws inspiration from classical East Asian antiquity."
Set in the magical land of Inkasisa, this beautiful fantasy is influenced by Bolivian culture and politics.
A woman adrift in a vast amount of space and time takes in a young boy.
Dhonielle Clayton's inspiration for "The Belles" came from how she felt about her body during her teenage years.
Tea, the protagonist, learns she can raise the dead.
Excellent epic fantasy set in a world based on Pre-Columbian Indigenous cultures
Based loosely on Ancient Roman society
When 16-year-old Deka's blood runs gold (a mark of impurity in her village), she makes the choice to join an army of gifted girls.
JADE CITY FONDA LEE
NEON YANG THE BLACK TIDES OF HEAVEN
THE POPPY WAR R.F. KUANG
ZEN CHO SORCERER TO THE CROWN
KAI ASHANTE WILSON A TASTE OF HONEY
THE VANISHED BIRDS SIMON JIMENEZ
ISABEL IBAÑEZ Woven in Moonlight
EACH OF US A DESERT Mark Oshiro
MEJIA WE SET THE DARK ON FIRE
BINTI THE COMPLETE TRILOGY NNEDI OKORAFOR
FIREHEART TIGER ALIETTE DE BODARD
THE FIFTH SEASON N.K. JEMISIN
The BONE WITCH RIN CHUPECO
BLACK SUN REBECCA ROANHORSE
CLAYTON THE BELLES
BLACK LEOPARD RED WOLF MARLON JAMES
THE EMPEROR'S WOLVES MICHELLE SAGARA
TOMI ADEYEMI CHILDREN OF BLOOD AND BONE
MARIE LU SKYHUNTER
DAUGHTERS OF NRI RENI K. AMAYO
REDEMPTION IN INDIGO KAREN LORD
JULIE C. DAO FOREST of a THOUSAND LANTERNS
SALADIN AHMED Throne of the Crescent Moon
KEN LIU THE GRACE OF KINGS
FAIZAL We Hunt the Flame
NAMINA FORNA THE GILDED ONES
SHADOW of the FOX JULIE KAGAWA
THE EMPRESS OF SALT AND FORTUNE NGHI VO
IFUEKO RAYBEARER
BROWN A SONG OF WRAITHS AND RUIN
AN EMBER IN THE ASHES SABAA TAHIR

SPECULATIVE FICTION: OTHER WORLDS

Often it can be easier to see or understand our society's problems clearly if they are put into a fresh context, or a whole other world.

This is the second book in the series!

Henry Holt and Company 2019 hardcover, design by Mallory Grigg, art by Sarah Jones

When Tomi Adeyemi was 18, she realized that all the stories she'd been writing for the last 12 years had white or biracial main characters, and that she "had internalized at a really young age that [B]lack people can't be in stories." So she made it her mission to write the fantasy tales she wanted to write, but with Black main characters, she says, "because I obviously have some severe self-esteem issues, and I figured them out through writing, so I can try and heal them through writing." Her hugely successful novel *Children of Blood and Bone*, the first of a trilogy, was published in 2018 when she was just 24.

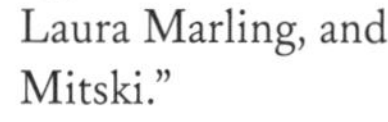

Harper Voyager 2019 paperback, design by Dominic Forbes, art by Jung Shan Chang

R. F. Kuang says her fantasy novel *The Poppy War* "grew out of a lot of childhood influences—*Ender's Game*, *Avatar: The Last Airbender*, and way too many Chinese wuxia TV dramas." To write her story of Rin, a proud, angry orphan trying to qualify for an elite military academy, Kuang studied Chinese history, particularly the wars of the twentieth century, as well as "Daoist mythology and Asian shamanism." She also asked her grandparents, since they lived through World War II, in China.

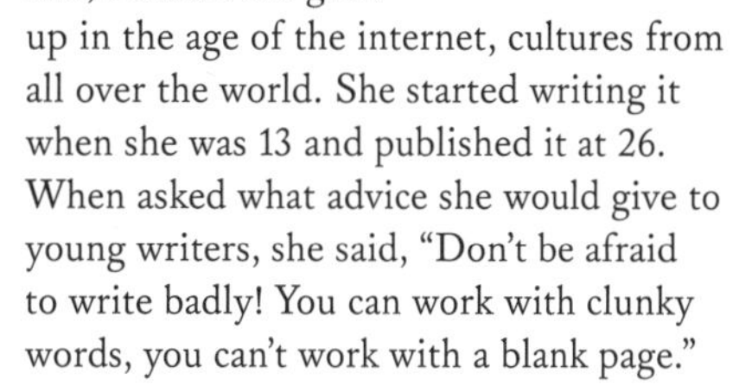

Jordan Ifueko is the daughter of Nigerian-immigrant parents, and the world she builds in her debut novel *Raybearer* was influenced by West African folklore, European fairy tales, and, because she grew up in the age of the internet, cultures from all over the world. She started writing it when she was 13 and published it at 26. When asked what advice she would give to young writers, she said, "Don't be afraid to write badly! You can work with clunky words, you can't work with a blank page."

Mark Oshiro—who lists in their bio a goal of petting every dog in the world—wrote *Each of Us a Desert* while listening to music nonstop. They specifically listened to artists Murder by Death, Florence + the Machine, and Fire From the Gods, "with some appearances from Solange, Laura Marling, and Mitski."

AWARD-WINNING BOOKS

These award-winning books have been universal connectors introducing readers to diverse stories, and many have broken historic barriers.

Scribner 2018 paperback, design by Helen Yentus, art by Jaya Miceli

SING, UNBURIED, SING

by Jesmyn Ward

2017 National Book Award for Fiction

The National Book Awards are given by the National Book Foundation to recognize literary excellence in America. Ward is the first woman to win two National Book Awards for Fiction; she also won for *Salvage the Bones* in 2011.

INTERIOR CHINATOWN

by Charles Yu

2020 National Book Award for Fiction

Vintage Books 2020 paperback, design by Linda Huang

Yu is the author of four books and his award-winning novel is being adapted into a Hulu television series.

HarperTeen 2018 hardcover, design by Erin Fitzsimmons art by Gabriel Moreno, photo by Amanda Rivas

THE POET X

by Elizabeth Acevedo

2019 Carnegie Medal

The CILIP Carnegie Medal is awarded by children's librarians for an outstanding book written in English for children and young people. Acevedo is the first writer of color to win the United Kingdom's oldest children's award in its 83-year history.

GIRL, WOMAN, OTHER

by Bernardine Evaristo

2019 Booker Prize

Penguin UK 2020 paperback, design by Richard Bravery, art by Karan Singh

The Booker Prize is a prestigious literary award for the best novel written in English and published in the United Kingdom or Ireland. Bernardine Evaristo is the first Black woman to win the Booker Prize.

AN AMERICAN MARRIAGE

by Tayari Jones

2019 Women's Prize for Fiction

Algonquin Books 2018 hardcover, design by Jaya Miceli

The Women's Prize for Fiction is the United Kingdom's annual book award celebrating and honoring fiction written by women.

W. W. Norton 2017 hardcover, design and art by Jaya Miceli

DO NOT SAY WE HAVE NOTHING

by Madeleine Thien

2016 Scotiabank Giller Prize

The Scotiabank Giller Prize is a literary award given to a Canadian author of a novel or short story collection published in English the previous year.

THE FIFTH SEASON

by N. K. Jemisin

2016 Hugo Award for Best Novel

Orbit 2015 paperback, design by Lauren Panepinto

The Hugo Award is science fiction's most prestigious prize. Jemisin is the first writer to win the Hugo Award three times in a row and the first to win top honors for every book in a series, the Broken Earth Trilogy.

Mariner Books 2019 paperback, design by Martha Kennedy, image by Donald Hamilton Fraser

INTERPRETER OF MALADIES

by Jhumpa Lahiri

2000 PEN/Hemingway Award for Debut Novel

The PEN/Hemingway Award for Debut Novel honors a debut fiction of exceptional merit by an American author who has not previously published a full-length book of fiction. Lahiri also won the 2000 Pulitzer Prize for Fiction for the same novel.

THE NICKEL BOYS

by Colson Whitehead

2020 Pulitzer Prize for Fiction

Doubleday 2019 hardcover, design by Oliver Munday, photo by Neil Libbert

The Pulitzer Prize for Fiction is awarded to an American author for distinguished fiction, preferably dealing with American life. Whitehead is the fourth writer in history to have won the Pulitzer for fiction twice. He won the prize in 2017 for *The Underground Railroad*.

HERE COMES THE SUN

by Nicole Dennis-Benn

2017 Lambda Literary Award for Lesbian Fiction

Liveright 2017 paperback, design and art by Jennifer Heuer

The Lambda Literary Awards (the "Lammys") are awarded yearly to the best lesbian, gay, bisexual, and transgender books. Dennis-Benn is a two-time Lambda Literary Award winner, also winning for her second novel, *Patsy*.

MYSTERIES & HORROR

These books run a wide gamut of subgenres, but they will all keep you questioning, wondering, figuring, puzzling, worrying, and eventually resolving, in some way or another.

Oyinkan Braithwaite was known for her poetry and short stories before she spent a year stressing about trying to write the perfect novel. Once she told herself to just write something "fun," she banged out the first draft of her best-selling book *My Sister, the Serial Killer* in one feverish month. When asked (by Ayọ̀bámi Adébáyọ̀, author of *Stay with Me*) about the difference between writing short pieces versus longer, Braithwaite said, "A novel requires stamina and grit. You need a certain kind of faith in yourself and in what you are doing to bang out 40,000-plus words."

Doubleday 2018 hardcover, design by Michael Windsor

Mexican Gothic was just Silvia Moreno-Garcia's working title for her novel set in a creepy mansion in a 1950s colonial hill town, but it stuck. This was partly because she found it amusing, "because when you are Latin American, everything you write is called magic realist by default, and that's the only thing you are allowed to write. I thought the title made it very clear that this is not magic realism and that we can write other stuff."

The Changeling is a horror-filled modern-day fairy tale about fatherhood, New York, and our need to be digitally liked. When asked about his inspiration, Victor LaValle said he was thinking about how dads sometimes get excessive credit just for showing up. He continues, "the nefarious side of all this is that being a 'good dad' is easy, being a 'good mother' is practically impossible. The par is ridiculously low for the former, impossibly high for the latter."

Hanover Square Press 2021 hardcover

Nadine Matheson is a criminal defense lawyer based in London. She has a comic book obsession and enjoys reading women's fiction and sci-fi, but crime fiction is her first love. *The Jigsaw Man* is her debut novel, inspired by the real-life case of Jeffrey Howe, who was murdered in 2009. Detective Inspector Anjelica Henley will return with a second book in the series.

In addition to writing, Tanarive Due teaches Black Horror and Afrofuturism at UCLA.

Marin's four-year-old son, Sebastian, is kidnapped by someone in a Santa suit three days before Christmas.

The Civil War dead become zombies and a young girl trains to fight them.

Stephen Graham Jones is a Blackfeet writer, and in this book he explores elk and deer mythology.

A 1990 classic, and Mosley's first published book

A thriller set on the Rosebud Indian Reservation in South Dakota where a vigilante searches for the source of a heroin influx

Two families in Los Angeles, one African American and the other Korean American, collide during the aftermath of the police shooting of a Black teenager.

AUTHORS RECOMMEND

BERNICE L. MCFADDEN

Author of *Sugar* and *The Book of Harlan*

Instagram: @bernicelmcfadden
Twitter: @queenazsa

Wandering in Strange Lands: A Daughter of the Great Migration Reclaims Her Roots
by Morgan Jerkins

Harper 2020 hardcover, design by Robin Bilardello

"This is a richly woven odyssey that should be read by everyone—but especially those people who have considered researching their family tree."

BRANDY COLBERT

Author of *The Only Black Girls in Town* and *Little & Lion*

Instagram/Twitter: @brandycolbert

Simon & Schuster 2020 hardcover, design by Lucy Ruth Cummins, art by Adriana Bellet

The Black Kids
by Christina Hammonds Reed

"*The Black Kids* by Christina Hammonds Reed is so many things I love: a witty and honest bildungsroman about a Black girl; a spot-on portrayal of how teens really act, speak, and think; and a love letter to Los Angeles that takes an insightful look at the 1992 uprising. This book is an ode to Black girls who feel like they don't quite fit in anywhere but try their best to stay true to themselves. I wish *The Black Kids* had existed when I was a teenager, and I am grateful to have it now."

SAUMYA DAVE

Author of *Well-Behaved Indian Women*

Instagram/Twitter: @saumyajdave

Girl in Translation
by Jean Kwok

Riverhead Books 2010 paperback design by Lisa Fyfe, photo by plainpicture/ballyscanlon

"I immediately fell in love with the excellent writing and moving plot in this book. Kimberly Chang and her mother emigrated from Hong Kong to Brooklyn, where Kimberly is a straight-A student during the day and a sweatshop worker at night. I enjoyed everything from the coming-of-age elements to the sweet mother-daughter relationship to the way Kimberly navigates poverty and private school. Highly recommend this for anyone wanting a story with a character you root for from beginning to end."

MELISSA RIVERO

Author of *The Affairs of the Falcóns*

Instagram: @melissarivero_
Twitter: @melissa_rivero

Grand Central Publishing 2021 hardcover, design by Sara Wood

What's Mine and Yours
by Naima Coster

"I absolutely love *What's Mine and Yours*. The novel centers on two families whose lives are impacted by a death early on in their lives, and later, the integration of a public school in North Carolina. The novel crisscrosses time, states, and the Atlantic Ocean as we see how these characters navigate the complexities of marriage, race, and family."

DE'SHAWN CHARLES WINSLOW

Author of *In West Mills*

Instagram: @deshawncharleswinslow

The Final Revival of Opal & Nev
by Dawnie Walton

37 Ink 2020 hardcover, design by David Litman

"In Dawnie Walton's debut novel, *The Final Revival of Opal & Nev,* we meet two talented singers from very opposite backgrounds, and a young, ambitious journalist seeking answers about her father's past. Opal and Nev's shared passion for music brings them together. But when racism and sexism are thrown into the mix, the characters are forced to choose a position. Written mostly in the style of interviews, this beautifully daring and evocative novel offers one shocking revelation after the next. I devoured this book."

NANCY JOOYOUN KIM

Author of *The Last Story of Mina Lee*

Instagram/Twitter: @njooyounkim

Kitchen Table 1988 paperback, design by Anne Cammet, calligraphy by Yoshikazu Yamada

Seventeen Syllables and Other Stories
by Hisaye Yamamato

"Born in 1921, Hisaye Yamamoto referred to herself as a "housewife, not a writer" with the same deadpan delivery found in her elegantly understated and deeply compassionate stories of Japanese American life. I first read *Seventeen Syllables* for a college course at a time when I struggled to imagine my own writing outside of the journal that I fed like a secret fire at night. Experiencing Yamamoto's work, which explored the complex silences within families and the struggles of women to create themselves, I caught a flicker of the burn of how I could be in this world—housewife or not."

Not the Girl You Marry — Andie J. Christopher (Berkley)

Adriana Herrera — Finding Joy

The Happy Ever After Playlist — USA Today Bestselling Author Abby Jimenez (Forever)

Real Men Knit — USA Today Bestselling Author Kwana Jackson (Berkley)

Nicola Yoon — The Sun Is Also a Star (Delacorte Press)

Fumbled — Alexa Martin (Berkley)

Sonali Dev — Recipe for Persuasion

The Kiss Quotient — Helen Hoang (Berkley)

Hidden Sins — Selena Montgomery

Crazy Rich Asians — Kevin Kwan (Anchor Books)

Junauda Petrus — The Stars and the Blackness Between Them (Dutton)

Eric Jerome Dickey — The Business of Lovers (Dutton)

The Worst Best Man — Mia Sosa (Avon Books)

Malinda Lo — Last Night at the Telegraph Club (Dutton)

Farrah Rochon — The Boyfriend Project (Forever)

A Princess in Theory — Alyssa Cole (Avon Books)

Royal Holiday — Jasmine Guillory, New York Times Bestselling Author (Berkley)

The Trouble with Hating You — Sajni Patel

To All the Boys I've Loved Before — Jenny Han

Kann — Let's Talk About Love (Swoon Reads)

You Had Me at Hola — Alexis Daria (Avon Books)

Ties That Tether — Jane Igharo (Berkley)

When Dimple Met Rishi — Menon (Simon Pulse)

Alisha Rai — The Right Swipe (Avon Books)

Amma K — A Love Story — Jenny Lee (Flatiron Books)

Get a Life, Chloe Brown — Talia Hibbert (Avon Books)

Indigo — Beverly Jenkins (Avon)

The Marriage Game — Sara Desai (Berkley)

High school sweethearts cross paths years later in the second novel in the Playbook series by Alexa Martin, the wife of a former NFL player.

A movie based on Nicola Yoon's excellent book, starring Yara Shahidi and Charles Melton, came out in 2019.

Kevin Kwan's immensely popular book was made into a 2018 hit movie. It was the first movie by a major Hollywood studio to feature a majority Asian cast since "The Joy Luck Club" in 1993.

Did you know that politician and voter rights advocate Stacey Abrams writes romance novels under the pen name Selena Montgomery?

A coming-of-age love story about two teen girls, one from Trinidad and one from Minneapolis

Adapted into the Netflix original series "Mismatched"

LOVE & ROMANCE

"Love is love is love is love is love is love is love is love, cannot be killed or swept aside," said Lin-Manuel Miranda. These books celebrate all kinds of love, and are full of great romance.

After learning that her daughter was on the autism spectrum, Helen Hoang conducted additional research and discovered that she was also autistic. Hoang used this discovery as her concept for *The Kiss Quotient* and entered the manuscript into the online mentoring program Pitch Wars, where it was selected by a published author who guided her through the publishing process. Her debut novel became an instant hit when it landed on shelves in 2018.

Sonali Dev discovered Jane Austen in the seventh grade via the TV series *Trishna*, an Indian adaptation of *Pride and Prejudice*. She is now writing a four-part series of contemporary romance novels based on the themes and lessons from her four favorite Austen novels—*Pride and Prejudice*, *Sense and Sensibility*, *Persuasion*, and *Emma*—centered on the Rajes, an Indian American family from California. *Recipe for Persuasion* is the second novel, and Dev says, "*Recipe for Persuasion* specifically is my homage to what I learned from *Persuasion*, which was that you can make mistakes, and there will always be a second chance."

William Morrow 2020 paperback, design and art by Kimberly Glyder

Berkley 2020 paperback, design by Emily Osborne, art by Fatima Baig

Jane Igharo discovered her love of writing after checking out *Some Nerve* by Jane Heller from the library. She became obsessed with the romance novel and knew at an early age that she wanted to be a writer. When asked to describe her novel in five words, Igharo said that *Ties That Tether* is a "a heart-warming, gut-wrenching culture-clash romance" and her inspiration for the novel came from wanting to "write a story about a woman who looked like me and shared similar experiences—dealing with my identity as an immigrant, dating men within and outside my ethnicity, and dealing with my family's expectations."

Talia Hibbert says she "lives in a bedroom full of books," and writes "steamy, diverse romance because [I believe] that people of marginalized identities need honest and positive representation." Hibbert's debut novel, *Get A Life, Chloe Brown*, is the first rom-com novel in the Brown Sisters trilogy and introduces us to a chronically ill computer geek whose near-death experience causes her to examine her life.

Avon 2019 paperback, design and art by Ashley Caswell

WRITING ROOMS

JASMINE GUILLORY

Author of *The Wedding Date* and *While We Were Dating*
Instagram: @jasminepics / Twitter: @thebestjasmine

"I know it is very bad to write in bed—bad for my posture and my nonexistent 'work/life balance,' but I do it anyway. I have a tiny office with a little desk and chair and yet I still write in bed because I'm used to it and it's cozy with a blanket over my shoulders and because if I'm stressed or overwhelmed, I can slump sideways on my pillows for a break. By my bed are two needlepoints from a friend: one with my favorite tiny bit of illustration and favorite quote from my favorite children's book (*The Little Engine that Could*) and one with a Beyoncé quote ('I'm a keep running cause a winner don't quit on themselves'). They keep me going."

Berkley 2021 paperback, design by Rita Frangie; art by Ayang Cempaka

Rodale Books 2016 hardcover, photo by Chantell Quernemoen

MOLLY YEH

Author of *Molly on the Range* and star of *Girl Meets Farm* on the Food Network
Instagram/Twitter: @mollyyeh

"This kitchen is in the farmhouse that my husband's grandparents built in the 1960s. We moved into it in 2014 and brightened it up by painting the original dark wood cabinets white and replacing the laminate countertops with butcher blocks, but a few little touches remain the same: The stove is original and, though she is tiny and electric, she is mighty! The hanging measuring spoons on the back wall near my refrigerator were also my grandmother-in-law's. The pantry used to consist of very short shelves that were on a slant so that you could add rows of cans and when you removed the front one, the next one rolled forward. There were handwritten labels on the shelves for various creamed soups up until last year when they were accidentally removed for filming purposes. A few more special touches in the kitchen that I love are the magnetic knife holder that my husband, Nick, made and presented to me when I handed in my first book manuscript; the triangle-shaped pull-out spice 'wedge' that Nick built; and the Bread Spot, which is the little cabinet underneath where I stand to film *Girl Meets Farm* and it's where I hide my coffee and snacks (usually bread)."

BOOKISH PEOPLE RECOMMEND

Little A 2018 hardcover, design by PEPE nymi

ANGELA MARÍA SPRING

Owner of Duende District

Instagram: @duendedistrict

Halsey Street
by Naima Coster

"A beautifully crafted novel by one of my favorite new voices in fiction, *Halsey Street* delivers the story of a young woman who reluctantly returns to her childhood Brooklyn home to care for her aging father, who owned a legendary local record store in their now nearly unrecognizable gentrifying neighborhood. She and her father both grapple with the ever-present shadow of her mother, who left them both years before to return to the Dominican Republic, while grasping to hold on to anything left that's familiar."

SEEMA VENNAM

Book reviewer

Instagram: @diversifyyourshelf

A Tale for the Time Being
by Ruth Ozeki

Viking 2013 hardcover, design by Jim Tierney

"This novel is an all-time favorite! It is complex and layered while staying fresh and unpretentious. The characters seem so real, and the book has a plethora of themes including family and loyalty, philosophy and loss, memory and erasure, ethical technology and war, climate change and spirituality, time and being (and not being), and . . . wow. For having multiple dark elements, it's still such a pleasure to read—entertaining, clever, and bright. There is SO MUCH to it that I feel I could read it 10 times and still make new connections. Ruth Ozeki is brilliant!"

Ballantine Books 2020 hardcover, design by Rachel Ake

SARAH COQUILLAT

Public health researcher and bookworm

Instagram: @bookishandblack

Here for It; Or, How to Save Your Soul in America: Essays
by R. Eric Thomas

"When I read nonfiction, I tend to gravitate toward memoirs or essay collections and this book is the perfect blend of both. In this collection, Thomas will have you laughing, crying, and reflecting on your own life. His writing is witty, honest, and deeply insightful. He touches on so many topics ranging from going viral by accident to the continued acceptance of one's true identity. If you cringe when you remember your first crush, if you've ever tried to help but made things worse, and if you've ever felt like you don't belong in a space that was supposed to be for you, then this book will surely resonate with you."

MALLORY WHITEDUCK

Professor of Indigenous political thought and bookstagrammer

Instagram: @nativegirlsreading

Love Medicine
by Louise Erdrich

Holt, Rinehart and Winston 1984 hardcover, design by Honi Werner

"*Love Medicine* brings reservation life to your bookshelf. Crack the cover and you'll hear whispers of community gossip and old ladies' laughter. You'll meet the everyday Native folks who make up an intergenerational family saga. It is a classic of Native literature, written by one of the field's heaviest hitters."

37 Ink 2015 paperback, design by Laywan Kwan, photo by Elton Anderson

SHANNON BLAND

Founder of Black Librarians

Instagram: @blacklibrarians

The Misadventures of Awkward Black Girl
by Issa Rae

"HILARIOUS! Issa Rae's quick wit and sarcasm, found in her character Jay of the web series form of *The Misadventures of Awkward Black Girl* and her self-titled character on HBO's *Insecure,* did not go missing in this book. In fact, I found that this book, a collection of essays portraying Issa Rae's actual life, to be even funnier. I see myself as an awkward Black girl, and with Issa Rae's struggles to fit in, love of 90s pop culture, chat room woes, liberating big chop, and other growing pains, this book was totally relatable. I recommend this book to not only awkward Black girls, but also to boys who have always been a little different from the rest of the crowd."

NICHOLAS ALEXANDER BROWN

COO for communication and outreach, Prince George's County Memorial Library System

Instagram: @frenchhorn88

Ecco 2014 hardcover, design by Allison Saltzman

The Prince of Los Cocuyos: A Miami Childhood
by Richard Blanco

"Richard Blanco made headlines as the first Latin and LGBTQIA+ poet to serve as inaugural poet, presenting at President Obama's second inauguration. *The Prince of Los Cocuyos* ("fireflies," in English) is his charming and poignant memoir that depicts his uniquely Cuban American childhood in Miami. Blanco artfully and humorously portrays how his intersecting cultures enabled him to fulfill his dreams and love himself and others."

CENTERING QUEER STORIES

Over the last decade, society has become more open and educated about sexuality and gender possibilities, and queerness has become more acceptable both socially and legally, but we should not be fooled into thinking everything is peachy. Recounting personal stories and weaving new ones normalizes them, centering queer experiences and demarginalizing lives.

How We Fight for Our Lives is Saeed Jones's powerful memoir about struggling to grow up Black and gay in the South, but it's also the story of his loving mother, a study on what it means to be a man, and a reflection on how to forge your identity as you find yourself. When asked about his mission as a writer, he said, "I want to be of use to people who, because of the way our country is, feel lonely. My mission would be to help people know they're not alone, whether they're a poet or a queer kid in the South, whether it's through a poem or a podcast or whatever."

About her debut novel, *Honey Girl*, Morgan Rogers says "I was writing the world as I saw it and also how it really is, which is a world in which queer people, especially queer people of color, live and breathe and survive for as long as we can." Rogers believes "found family" or "chosen family" is an important component of the varied queer experience and that "you need queer friends and queer friends that feel like family because those are the people you lean on and learn from and support on your respective journeys."

Park Row 2021 paperback, design by Gigi Lau, art by Poppy Magda

Activist and scholar Gloria E. Anzaldúa, one of the first openly queer Chicana writers, was born in Texas just north of Mexico, and knew what it felt like to be marginalized, in between acceptable places and acceptable identities. *Borderlands/La Frontera: The New Mestiza* is her 1987 argument that borders are fertile places of mixing and crossover, not boundaries and walls. In her book she blurs all the lines: mixing poetry and prose, English and Spanish, memoir and history.

Aunt Lute Books 1987 paperback, art by Pamela Wilson

In the Dream House is a genre-bending memoir written in the second person, in which Carmen Maria Machado traces the arc of her relationship with her abusive ex-girlfriend and their life in a small house in Indiana. Each chapter focuses on a different style metaphor, including one that acts as a wonky "Choose Your Own Adventure" story, gaslighting the reader. It blends both scholarship and folklore to address queer domestic abuse, something rarely written about.

A memoir about being a queer Muslim immigrant and trying to make space for yourself in the world
Samra Habib We Have Always Been Here Viking
Silvera They Both Die at the End Harper Teen
They do, but no more than we all do.
Long Live the Tribe of Fatherless Girls
T Kira Madden
A memoir about being a queer, biracial teenager in Boca Raton, Florida
Under the Udala Trees Chinelo Okparanta
Real Life Brandon Taylor Riverhead Books
A middle-grade novel about a gay Indian American boy finding himself
Pancholy The Best at It B+B
Granta We the Animals Justin Torres
Kilodavis/DeSimone My Princess Boy
Morgan Rogers Honey Girl
Machado In the Dream House
In 2019, Mock signed a historic deal with Netflix, making her the first trans person to sign a production pact with a major studio.
Baldwin's second novel, written mostly while living in France, is the story of an American man and an Italian bartender who meet in a Parisian bar.
James Baldwin Giovanni's Room Vintage
How We Fight for Our Lives Saeed Jones
Here Comes the Sun Nicole Dennis-Benn
akwaeke emezi Pet
A young adult novel about a trans girl who befriends a monster
Redefining Realness Janet Mock
Callender Felix Ever After B+B
Jacqueline Woodson The House You Pass on the Way Puffin
Sáenz Aristotle and Dante Discover the Secrets of the Universe Simon & Schuster
Atta the Black Flamingo B+B
Fairest Meredith Talusan
The Henna Wars adiba jaigirdar
Zami A New Spelling of My Name Audre Lorde
Carolina de Robertis Cantoras Knopf
Curato Flamer Henry Holt
Tamaki Valero-O'Connell Laura Dean Keeps Breaking Up with Me :01 First Second
Johnson All Boys Aren't Blue FSG
Borderlands/La Frontera Gloria Anzaldúa
Wang The Prince and the Dressmaker :01 First Second
A young adult novel about romance between rival henna artists
A graphic novel about summer camp, sexuality, and self-acceptance

BEAUTIFULLY ILLUSTRATED COVERS

Often a designer will have a vision for a cover that features a particular image, and in a particular style. They might find an existing illustration and buy permission to use it on the cover, or they might find a suitable artist and commission them to create something perfect.

Jacaranda Books
2019 paperback

THE MARROW THIEVES

by Cherie Dimaline

UK edition art by Chief Lady Bird

Instagram: @chiefladybird

Chief Lady Bird is a Chippewa and Potawatomi artist, illustrator, educator, and community activist living in Toronto, Ontario.

PATRON SAINTS OF NOTHING

by Randy Ribay

design by Dana Li, art by Jor Ros

Instagram: @danalidesign @jor.ros

Kokila
2020 hardcover

Li is a designer for Catapult/Counterpoint Press. She also designed the cover for *City of Saints & Thieves* by Natalie C. Anderson and *The First Rule of Punk* by Celia C. Pérez.

Little, Brown
2018 hardcover

TYLER JOHNSON WAS HERE

by Jay Coles

design by Marcie Lawrence, art by Charlotte Day

Instagram: @marcielawrence.design @charlottepaints

Lawrence, an associate art director at Abrams, notes, "I can count on one hand the African American book cover designers–of which I am one of–in the industry, and I think there should be more representation in sales, marketing, and publicity in addition to editorial departments."

A CUBAN GIRL'S GUIDE TO TEA AND TOMORROW

by Laura Taylor Namey

design by Karyn S. Lee, art by Andi Porretta

Instagram: @karynslee @andi.porretta

Atheneum
2020 hardcover

Lee is also an illustrator herself!

Farrar, Straus and Giroux
2020 hardcover

ALL BOYS AREN'T BLUE

by George M. Johnson

design by Cassie Gonzales, art by Charly Palmer

Instagram: @casacassie

Gonzales says that "the main goal of a book cover is to sort of distill down the purpose of the book into one recognizable rectangle."

A SONG BELOW WATER

by Bethany C. Morrow

design by Lesley Worrell, art by Alex Cabal

Instagram:
@lesleyworrell/@acaballz

Tor Teen
2020 hardcover

Worrell also designed the covers for *See No Color* by Shannon Gibney and *Auma's Long Run* by Eucabeth Odhiambo.

Inkyard Press
2019 hardcover

DEAR HAITI, LOVE ALAINE

by Maika Moultie and Maritza Moultie

design by Gigi Lau, art by Lord Kpuri

Instagram:
@lau.gigi.lau/@lord_kpuri

Lau is an art director at Harlequin. She also designed the covers for *Honey Girl* by Morgan Rogers and Francina Simone's *Smash It!*

FAT CHANCE, CHARLIE VEGA

by Crystal Maldonado

design by Chelsea Hunter, art by Ericka Lugo

Instagram: @seehunter
@erilu.jpg

Holiday House
2021 hardcover

Hunter started out designing nonfiction books but then switched to fiction for young people. Lugo is based in Puerto Rico.

Dial Books
2019 hardcover

DARIUS THE GREAT IS NOT OKAY

by Adib Khorram

design by Samira Iravani, art by Adams Carvalho

Instagram:
@suchdainties
@adamscarvalho

Iravani says her favorite components for a new project are "an editor with a clear vision for the cover, and a story I could really sink my teeth into."

HIJABISTAN

by Sabyn Javeri

design by Amit Malhotra, art by Samya Arif

Instagram: @samyaarif

Harper India
2020 paperback

Malhotra is a senior designer at HarperCollins Publishers India, and Arif is a Karachi-based artist and illustrator.

About Kiera, a 17-year-old high school student and online game developer. You will wish you could play the game she creates.
There is also a graphic novel adaptation of Rivera's book, with art by Celia Moscote!
Two estranged sisters have to swap identities when one is diagnosed with cancer and needs to use the other's health insurance.
David Yoon is married to novelist Nicola Yoon and he drew the illustrations for her No. 1 "New York Times" best seller "Everything, Everything".
Cynthia Leitich Smith is a citizen of the Muscogee (Creek) Nation, and this book is about "dating while Native."
Shirin, a sixteen-year-old Muslim girl, navigates life and love while grappling with being stereotyped in a post 9/11 America.
A debut novel about a Black family battling racial injustice and the American criminal justice system
NIC STONE Dear Martin CROWN
GABBY RIVERA JULIET TAKES A BREATH DIAL
RANDY RIBAY PATRON SAINTS OF NOTHING Kokila
ACEVEDO WITH THE FIRE ON HIGH HARPER TEEN
SLAY MORRIS
THE MARROW THIEVES CHERIE DIMALINE
CANDICE ILOH EVERY BODY LOOKING DUTTON
Medina • Robinson • Jennings I AM ALFONSO JONES TU BOOKS
CHRISTINA HAMMONDS REED The BLACK KIDS SIMON & SCHUSTER
ZOBOI SALAAM PUNCHING THE AIR B+B
Choi YOLK Simon & Schuster
BROWN BLACK GIRL UNLIMITED
JOHNSON YOU SHOULD SEE ME IN A CROWN SCHOLASTIC PRESS
DAVID YOON FRANKLY in LOVE Putnam
BOULLEY FIREKEEPER'S DAUGHTER HENRY HOLT
SMITH Hearts UNBROKEN
MÉNDEZ FURIA
JASON REYNOLDS LONG WAY DOWN
JACKSON GROWN KT
THOMAS THE HATE U GIVE B+B
CHEE WE ARE NOT FREE HMH
KIM JOHNSON THIS IS MY AMERICA RANDOM HOUSE
ADIB KHORRAM DARIUS THE GREAT IS NOT OKAY
MALORIE BLACKMAN Noughts + Crosses
MAHOGANY L. BROWNE CHLORINE SKY CROWN
SAMIRA AHMED INTERNMENT LITTLE, BROWN
Stacey Lee THE DOWNSTAIRS GIRL Putnam
A VERY LARGE EXPANSE OF SEA TAHEREH MAFI HARPER
Apple Skin to the Core BY ERIC GANSWORTH LQ LEVINE QUERIDO
S.K. ALI LOVE FROM A TO Z SALAAM READS

COMING OF AGE

Being a teenager, that weird turbulent time when you start to figure out who you are and change from child to adult, is always intense: sometimes joyful and often painful—especially for your heart.

Jason Reynolds, author of *Long Way Down*, usually does dozens of in-person book readings and signings for young people every year. "I can talk directly to them in a way that I know they're going to relate to because I am them, and I still feel like them," he says. In 2020, as the newly appointed National Ambassador for Young People's Literature, he would have done even more had there not been a global pandemic. Instead, he and the Library of Congress created the "Write. Right. Rite." video series. In each biweekly episode, Reynolds touches on topics like "creativity, connection, and imagination," and then provides a prompt to inspire creative activities, both fun and challenging.

Henry Holt 2021 hardcover, design by Rich Deas, art by Moses Lunham

Angeline Boulley first thought about the story for her debut novel when she was just 18, but didn't start writing it until many years later. It then took her a decade to finish, but that time paid off: twelve publishing houses bid on it and it sold to Macmillan for seven figures. Boulley was 55 when *Firekeeper's Daughter* was published in 2021, and Barack and Michelle Obama's production company, Higher Ground, acquired the rights to create a Netflix original series based on it.

Scholastic Press 2020 hardcover, design by Stephanie Yang

Leah Johnson says that "Black joy is at the heart of all the work I do. I want to capture Black girls, particularly Black queer girls, as their whole selves." *You Should See Me in a Crown* is a totally joy-filled novel about high school, prom, dreams, and first love that will give you happy tears at the end.

Simon & Schuster 2020 paperback, design by Lucy Ruth Cummins, art by Mary Kate McDermitt

Love from A to Z is story of two Muslim teens—one an American of Pakistani and West Indian descent, and the other a Canadian of Chinese and Finnish descent—who meet on a plane to Doha, Qatar. The author, S. K. Ali, who wears hijab, also co-authored *The Proudest Blue*—a children's picture book about a girl who overcomes being bullied for wearing hijab—with Ibtihaj Muhammad, who in 2016 became the first American woman to compete in the Olympics in hijab (and won a medal doing it).

INFLUENTIAL BOOK PEOPLE

CHARNAIE GORDON

Diversity & Inclusion expert
Here Wee Read, LLC

Instagram: @HereWeeRead

"If people are committed to change for a better and equal world for children of the next generation, they should be open to exposing kids to a wide range of people, experiences, abilities, races, and cultures.

As a parent, my goal is to present my children with a full spectrum of Black and brown characters in a variety of books. I want their experiences of story and representations of the world to include people of color, people they can imagine being like—people like Oprah Winfrey, Barack Obama, Misty Copeland, and Michelle Obama—or fictional characters with whom they can identify.

Representation in books truly does matter. When children of color read books written by BIPOC authors and see illustrations by BIPOC illustrators, their beautiful reflections are shown back to them on the pages. This reinforces the fact that if they can see it, they can be it. When white children read books by BIPOC authors they are given a window to peek inside and learn about people of different skin tones and cultures. This not only builds empathy, but it also shows them that people of color can win too and be the hero or heroine of a story."

ALICIA TAPIA

Creator of the Bibliobicicleta

Instagram: @bibliobicicleta

"The Bibliobicicleta of San Francisco—a pop-up traveling trade library bicycle—was crowdfunded in 2013 by a diverse group of individuals who believe in the beauty of accessible books, bikes, and knowledge. Books expand our minds. They open our imaginations, deepen our understanding of ourselves and others, and allow us to face the issues humankind has faced in the past and contends with in the present. They offer building blocks to a better future.

Where are we from and where are we going? Simply read some books and apply it to what you see. There is no 'best' way, nor one solution to all problems for all people despite what white, Western, patriarchal society has told us.

These books have affected my worldview as a Filipina-Mexicana who grew up in Hawai'i, now living on Native American land. I possess a deep respect for Indigenous ways of knowing and diverse perspectives.

The best part of Bibliobicicleta is the people it brings together. Every human is a deep well of knowledge with such a diverse range of experiences and ways of knowing and seeing our world. Rainbows are beautiful because of the diversity and depth of colors; make sure your reading is as beautiful or you might miss it!"

MIDDLE GRADE

The first books we read on our own stick with us more than any others, so it's important that they show the world as it truly is: filled with all kinds of people with all kinds of stories. These are the books that you hug to your chest after finishing.

Kwame Alexander's *The Crossover*, a novel in verse about two brothers who love basketball, won the 2015 Newbery Medal. When interviewed about why he makes sure to write in a way that's accessible and engaging, Alexander said, "I went through a phase in middle school where . . . I loathed [reading] because I was being forced to do it. . . . I think that books are like amusement parks, and sometimes we have to let the kids choose the rides. And I wasn't being given that opportunity to ride, to find my groove."

During his book-hating phase, Alexander played a lot of basketball and football, and eventually re-found his love of reading through books about sports, like Muhammad Ali's autobiography, "The Greatest: My Own Story."

As the only Asian kid in her elementary school, Grace Lin spent much of her time trying to forget she was Asian. Now as an author-illustrator, she makes the books she wishes she'd had as a child. She feels that it's critical for children to have books on their shelves that are both windows to the outside world and mirrors showing them how beautiful they are. As she explains, "Books erase bias, they make the uncommon everyday, and the mundane exotic. A book makes all cultures universal."

Little, Brown 2009 hardcover, art by Grace Lin

For *The Barren Grounds*, the first book in his Misewa Saga trilogy, David A. Robertson was inspired by C. S. Lewis's Narnia, but approached it through the lens of traditional Cree stories. Morgan and Eli, two Cree foster kids, travel through a portal to a cold and barren land called Askî, populated by a community of talking animals in need of their help.

In his autobiographical middle-grade novel *Everything Sad Is Untrue*, Daniel Nayeri shares his family's journey from Iran to America. During his early childhood in Iran, his mom converted to Christianity, which was a crime, and they were forced to escape. They spent time as refugees before immigrating to Oklahoma. Nayeri shares that he became a writer because "the first question you end up getting asked is, What are you doing here? And you end up having to tell the story over and over again, which is sort of where my love of storytelling began." The novel won the 2021 Michael L. Printz Award for Excellence in Young Adult Literature. Nayeri, a former pastry chef, is also the publisher of Odd Dot, an imprint of Macmillan Children's Publishing Group.

Jacqueline Woodson was the 2018–2019 National Ambassador for Young People's Literature.
A young girl tries to make a deal with a magical tiger straight out of Korean folklore.
This won the 2020 National Book Award for Young People's Literature.
Twelve-year-old Malú starts a punk band full of misfits at her middle school and learns how to be herself.
The Portland protagonist, Ryan Hart, was inspired by Beverly Cleary's Ramona.
The first sentence of this book is "My gym shorts burrow into my butt crack like a frightened groundhog."
About Mia Tang, who lives in a motel and helps manage the front desk
Jewell Parker Rhodes GHOSt BOYS
NAYERI EVERYTHING SAD IS UNTRUE
JACQUELINE WOODSON Before the Ever After
Willing McManis Sorrell INDIAN NO MORE
BRANDY COLBERT THE ONLY BLACK GIRLS IN TOWN
YANG AMERICAN BORN CHINESE
ROBERTSON THE BARREN GROUNDS
Grace Lin WHERE THE MOUNTAIN MEETS THE MOON
CELIA C. PÉREZ THE FIRST RULE OF PUNK
TAE KELLER When You Trap a Tiger
Lai Inside Out & Back Again
WATSON WAYS TO MAKE SUNSHINE
TAHEREH MAFI FURTHERMORE
CRAFT NEW KID
DAY I CAN MAKE THIS PROMISE
Higuera LUPE WONG WON'T DANCE
Williams Genesis Begins Again
ORTEGA GHOST SQUAD
RYAN Esperanza Rising
reynolds GHOST
ALEXANDER THE CROSSOVER
WILLIAMS-GARCIA ONE CRAZY SUMMER
MEJIA PAOLA SANTIAGO AND THE RIVER OF TEARS
PARK PRAIRIE LOTUS
WARGA OTHER WORDS FOR HOME
Aisha Saeed AMAL UNBOUND
DRAPER STELLA by STARLIGHT
YANG FRONT DESK
Roll of Thunder, Hear My Cry TAYLOR
CALLENDER KING AND THE DRAGONFLIES
Ramée A Good Kind of Trouble
OH SPIRIT HUNTERS
GLASER THE VANDERBEEKERS of 141st STREET
BROWNE / TAYLOR WOKE A YOUNG POET'S CALL TO JUSTICE
CHANANI Pashmina

AMAZING ILLUSTRATORS

Picture books, whether for kids or grown-ups, combine words and pictures to tell a story in a much more impactful way than it could be told with only one or the other. Often the images hold extra clues to what is really happening, adding a layer of emotional data that really brings the story to life.

SEAN QUALLS

Instagram: @sean_qualls

Grandad Mandela
by Ambassador Zindzi Mandela, Zazi Mandela, and Ziwelene Mandela

Frances Lincoln
2018 hardcover

Qualls often collaborates with his wife, author-illustrator Selina Alko. They worked together on their 2015 kids' book *The Case for Loving: The Fight for Interracial Marriage*.

RAFAEL LÓPEZ

Instagram: @rafael_l61

The Day You Begin
by Jacqueline Woodson

Nancy Paulsen Books
2018 hardcover

López co-founded the Urban Art Trail movement in San Diego's East Village, creating a series of large murals in public spaces such as schools, hospitals, and under freeways. He then illustrated a book about how it brought the neighborhood together, called *Maybe Something Beautiful*, written by F. Isabel Campoy and Theresa Howell.

Orchard Books
2020 hardcover

BRYAN COLLIER

All Because You Matter
by Tami Charles

Collier starts with a storyboard, but the end result is usually very different. "Something else happens in the process of making the art. . . . New ideas come into play that seem to be more important to me or more profound to the text. I follow that. . . . I leave that door open to make sure it happens. . . . I want to see what happens on the fly."

Roaring Brook Press
2020 hardcover

MICHAELA GOADE

Instagram: @michaelagoade

We Are Water Protectors
by Carole Lindstrom

Goade, a member of the Tlingit & Haida Indian Tribes of Alaska, was the first Indigenous illustrator (and first BIPOC woman!) to win a Caldecott medal, in 2021 for *We Are Water Protectors*.

HATEM ALY

Instagram:
@metahatem

The Proudest Blue
by Ibtihaj Muhammad
and S. K. Ali

Little, Brown
2019 hardcover

Aly was born in Egypt and now lives in New Brunswick, Canada

DANIELLE DANIEL

Orca Book Publishers
2017 hardcover

Instagram:
@danielledaniel

You Hold Me Up
by Monique
Gray Smith

In addition to both illustrating books and writing her own, in 2019, Daniel founded A Mighty Village, "a national children's literacy initiative to help promote a more inclusive society." (mightyvillage.ca)

LEO ESPINOSA

HarperCollins
2020 hardcover

Instagram:
@studioespinosaworks

A Girl Named Rosita: The Story of Rita Moreno: Actor, Singer, Dancer, Trailblazer!
by Anika Aldamuy
Denise

Espinosa is from Bogotá, Colombia, and now lives in Salt Lake City, Utah.

LUISA URIBE

Instagram:
@lupencita

Your Name Is a Song
by Jamilah
Thompkins-Bigelow

The Innovation Press
2020 hardcover

When author Thompkins-Bigelow was asked what she felt the first time she saw Uribe's illustration for the cover of *Your Name Is a Song,* she said, "Joy. I felt absolute joy."

GORDON C. JAMES

Instagram:
@gordoncjamesfineart

I Am Every Good Thing
by Derrick Barnes

Nancy Paulsen Books
2020 hardcover

The artist based the boy on the cover of *I Am Every Good Thing* on his son Gabriel.

Ningiukulu (formerly Ningeokuluk) Teevee is an Inuit artist and writer born in Kinngait (formerly Cape Dorset), off Baffin Island.

About an American girl connecting with her Babi Ba (grandmother) and her Indian heritage

Harpreet is a young Sikh boy who wears a different color patka (traditional head covering) depending on how he's feeling.

A beautiful book about learning to love what makes you, you

The audiobook is narrated by Blue Ivy Carter, daughter of Beyoncé and Jay-Z!

APONTE ACROSS THE BAY
PATEL PRIYA DREAMS OF MARIGOLDS & MASALA BEAVER'S POND PRESS
The Pencil Avingaq · Vsetula · Chua INHABIT
THOMPKINS-BIGELOW URIBE YOUR Name IS A Song
WALKER & HARRISON NANA AKUA GOES TO SCHOOL
Alego Ningeokuluk Teevee
Lindstrom Goade WE ARE Water PROTECTORS
WATSON · ROBINSON Harlem's Little Blackbird
JERRY PINKNEY THE LION & THE MOUSE Little, Brown
robinson you matter atheneum
KELKAR ✱ MARLEY THE MANY COLORS OF HARPREET SINGH STERLING
ROBERTSON / FLETT When We Were Alone HIGHWATER PRESS
Isabel Quintero · Zeke Peña MY PAPI HAS A MOTORCYCLE Kokila
Medina · Sánchez EVELYN DEL REY IS MOVING AWAY Candlewick Press
OGE MORA SATURDAY
Maillard Martínez-Neal FRY BREAD
NYONG'O ✱ HARRISON SULWE Simon & Schuster
COZBI A. CABRERA Me & Mama SIMON & SCHUSTER
Vanessa Brantley-Newton JUST LIKE ME Knopf
Little You Richard Van Camp Julie Flett
TOO MANY MANGOS Paikai · Robinson ISLAND HERITAGE PUBLISHING
GRACE LIN A BIG Mooncake for Little Star
Sweetest Kulu Kalluk · Neonakis INHABIT MEDIA
HARRIS GONZÁLEZ KAMALA and MAYA'S BIG IDEA
Jacqueline Ayer The Paper-Flower Tree Enchanted Lion Books
Schofield-Morrison Morrison I GOT THE RHYTHM
Ahmed · Burrington MAE AMONG THE STARS HARPER
Juana Martinez-Neal ALMA and How She Got Her Name CANDLEWICK PRESS
Phi · Bui A Different Pond capstone
Morales Dreamers Neal Porter Books / Holiday House
Katrina Goldsaito Julia Kuo THE SOUND OF SILENCE
ZHANG · CHUA AMY WU and the PERFECT BAO
RITA LORRAINE HUBBARD & OGE MORA THE OLDEST STUDENT
Sonia Sotomayor · Rafael López JUST ASK! Philomel
DERRICK BARNES · GORDON C. JAMES I AM EVERY GOOD THING Nancy Paulsen Books
PAK GOODBYE SUMMER, HELLO AUTUMN HENRY HOLT
Matt de la Peña · Christian Robinson LAST STOP ON MARKET STREET Putnam
TONATIUH SEPARATE IS NEVER EQUAL ABRAMS
FIELDS + MOISES HONEYSMOKE
JACQUELINE WOODSON RAFAEL LÓPEZ THE DAY YOU BEGIN NANCY PAULSEN BOOKS
CHOI THE NAME JAR KNOPF
You Hold Me Up Monique Gray Smith and Danielle Daniel

BYERS | BOBO I AM ENOUGH
Ho · Ho Eyes that Kiss in the Corners HARPER
Pizzoli/Fabiani TALLULAH THE TOOTH FAIRY CEO FSG
Matthew A. Cherry Vashti Harrison Hair Love Kokila
IBTIHAJ MUHAMMAD / HATEM ALY THE PROUDEST BLUE
Saad · Sobhy Eid Breakfast at Abuela's Ahili'i/Tsong
PELE FINDS A HOME

Worried that her name is too strange for her classmates, Unhei asks for their help picking a new one.

Gabrielle Ahili'i has written a series of board book adaptations of Hawaiian legends.

KIDS' PICTURE BOOKS

Every child should be able to recognize themselves in books. The Cooperative Children's Book Center at the University of Wisconsin conducts an annual survey on diversity in children's and YA literature, and their 2019 review shows that things are improving, but incredibly slowly. Books about white protagonists made up 41.8% of the 3,717 books reviewed, and animals (or "other") made up 29.2%. Only 11.9% had Black main characters, 8.7% Asian, 5.3% Latinx, and only 1% Native.

Dreamers is a memoir in poetic picture book form about Yuyi Morales's emigration from Mexico to the United Sates with her baby son. She was still learning English and discovering that she could read picture books to Kelly via the pictures alone, which she says, "was like magic. It is like magic! I want to make sure that in my books, you can read the story even if you can't completely make out the text." Morales includes drawings of many of those books in her illustrations, paying tribute to the magicians before her.

Morales drew the art for "Dreamers" with a nib pen that once belonged to Maurice Sendak, given to her by Lynn Caponera, president and treasurer of the Maurice Sendak Foundation.

Enchanted Lion
2017 hardcover

Jacqueline Ayer was born in the Bronx in 1930 to Jamaican parents. She worked as a fashion illustrator in Paris, then traveled around Asia with her husband before settling in Bangkok where they had two daughters. She published eight children's books while there, and then later worked as a textile and product designer in India, New York, and London. Her books were out of print until the publisher Enchanted Lion reissued two of them in 2017.

Meena Harris, author of *Kamala and Maya's Big Idea*, is the CEO of Phenomenal, a lifestyle brand that brings awareness to various social causes. Harris, who is also a lawyer, began her career in tech at Facebook. She is the daughter of Maya Harris and the niece of Kamala Harris, the Vice President of the United States.

Kevin Noble Maillard, a law professor, journalist, and member of the Seminole Nation, Mekusukey Band, wrote *Fry Bread* when he couldn't find enough books by Native authors to read to his young son. His elderly aunts used to be his family's fry bread makers, but when they died, he stepped up and learned to do it himself.

Roaring Brook Press
2019 hardcover, art by
Juana Martinez-Neal

Fry bread is made by deep frying flat rounds of wheat dough in oil so that they puff up and turn golden. People top them with either savory or sweet toppings, including beans, meat, jam, and honey.

AMAZING AUTHOR-ILLUSTRATORS

The visual geniuses shown here not only illustrate books for other writers, but also both write and illustrate books all on their own. And while these author-illustrators happen to mostly create books for children, there are many who also create picture books for grown-ups. But remember: It's totally okay for adults to buy and love kids' books too.

CHRISTIAN ROBINSON

Instagram: @theartoffun

You Matter

Atheneum Books 2020 hardcover

Robinson often works in a combination of paint and collage, and collaged pieces of painted paper to make the images for his books.

Little, Brown 2009 hardcover

JERRY PINKNEY

Instagram: @jerrypinkneystudio

The Lion & the Mouse

Pinkney is a legend in picture book illustration, and he is known for updating old fables and fairy tales to modern times. The cover of *The Lion & the Mouse* is remarkable for its lack of title and author, featuring only the lion's very expressive face.

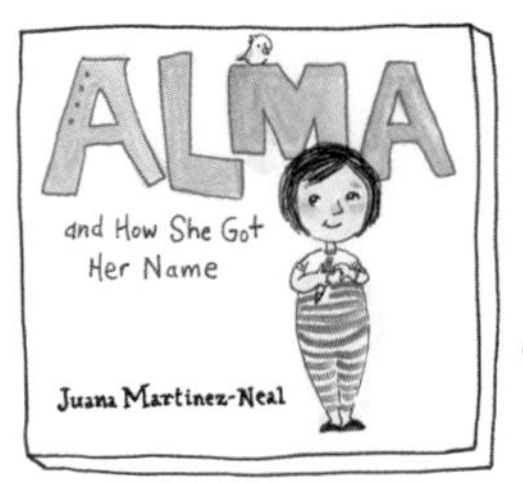

Candlewick 2018 hardcover

JUANA MARTINEZ-NEAL

Instagram: @juanamartinezn

Alma and How She Got Her Name

Martinez-Neal was born in Lima, Peru, and now lives in Arizona. She works in acrylic paint, colored pencils, and graphite.

OGE MORA

Instagram: @oge_mora

Thank You, Omu!

Little, Brown 2018 hardcover

Mora attended Rhode Island School of Design and landed her first book deal while still a senior there.

VASHTI HARRISON

Instagram: @vashtiharrison

Little, Brown
2017 hardcover

Little Leaders: Bold Women in Black History

Harrison has an MFA in film and video from California Institute of the Arts and made several experimental films before focusing on book illustration.

VANESSA BRANTLEY-NEWTON

Instagram: @vanessabrantleynewton

Knopf
2020 hardcover

Just Like Me

Brantley-Newton illustrates her own books and those written by others, including Derrick Barnes's *The King of Kindergarten*.

JAVAKA STEPTOE

Instagram: @javakasteptoe

Little, Brown 2016 hardcover, design by Phil Caminiti

Radiant Child: The Story of Young Artist Jean-Michel Basquiat

Steptoe won the 2017 Caldecott Medal for this book.

COZBI A. CABRERA

Instagram: @cozbi

Me & Mama

Cabrera also makes lovely cloth dolls called Muñecas.

Simon & Schuster
2020 hardcover

JULIE FLETT

Instagram: @julie__flett

Birdsong

Greystone Kids
2019 hardcover

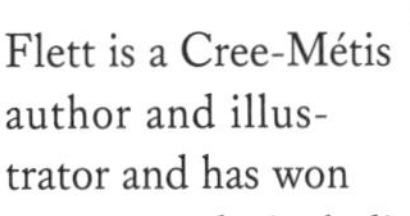

Flett is a Cree-Métis author and illustrator and has won many awards, including the 2017 Governor General's Award for Young People's Literature in Canada.

KADIR NELSON

Instagram: @kadirnelson

Balzer + Bray
2011 hardcover

Heart and Soul: The Story of America and African Americans

Nelson has illustrated over 30 children's books, and he won the Caldecott Medal in 2020 for his work on *The Undefeated,* written by Kwame Alexander.

BELOVED BOOKSTORES

UNCLE BOBBIE'S COFFEE & BOOKS

Philadelphia, Pennsylvania, USA
Instagram: @unclebobbies

Uncle Bobbie's is a place for everyone. The coffee shop and bookstore hosts free author talks, workshops, weekly story times for children, and back-to-school supply drives. Customers can sit at the bar and enjoy the delicious coffee and food selection or relax in the cozy "feels like home" lounge areas. There's so much to love about this space. Located in Philadelphia's Germantown neighborhood, Uncle Bobbie's was founded by Marc Lamont Hill in 2017 to provide underserved communities access to books and to create a space where everyone feels valued.

RED PLANET BOOKS & COMICS

Albuquerque, New Mexico, USA
Instagram: @redplanetbnc

Lee Francis IV, a member of the Laguna Pueblo, opened Red Planet in 2017 after he founded and hosted a successful Indigenous Comic Con in Albuquerque in 2016. Red Planet Comics, an independent publisher of Native comics, is the only Native comic-book shop in the world. "We don't carry anything in the shop that represents Native folks in a negative way," says Francis. He also helped find up-and-coming artists to join Marvel Comics when they assembled Native artists and writers for *Marvel Voices: Indigenous Voices #1,* an anthology that revisited some of its Native characters.

EYESEEME AFRICAN AMERICAN CHILDREN'S BOOKSTORE

St. Louis, Missouri, USA
Instagram: @eyeseeme_bookstore

When Pamela and Jeffrey Blair, owners and founders of EyeSeeMe Bookstore, began homeschooling their children in grade school, they noticed a void in the curriculum—a lack of books about African American history, heroes, and accomplishments. After extensive research, they opened EyeSeeMe in 2015 in order to help bridge the cultural divide, so that African American children could benefit from exposure to literature that respectfully mirrors themselves, their culture, and their families. The Blairs believe "children need to have Black role models and need to have a sense of history in order to understand who they are and build their self-esteem. When children see the many contributions that people that look like them have accomplished and have contributed to the world, they begin to believe in their own limitless potential." EyeSeeMe is the only children's bookstore devoted exclusively to promoting positive African American images and African American history while advocating for academic excellence. During the school year, the store hosts book fairs, making sure that all children have a healthy perspective about the contributions of African Americans.

COOKING & BAKING

These are the cookbooks you'll use every day, the ones that will get stained and spattered and wrinkly on the edges. Some of them will meet your therapy-baking needs, while others will teach you to make healthy comfort food for dinner.

Edna Lewis was cooking slow, seasonal, farm-to-table food and writing about it long before most anyone else. She was born in a small Virginia town founded by freed slaves (including her grandfather), became a famous chef and restaurant owner in New York, and eventually returned to the South. *In Pursuit of Flavor* was her third cookbook, first published in 1988 and reissued in 2019.

Bryant Terry, the chef-in-residence at the Museum of the African Diaspora in San Francisco, aims to show that veganism is for everyone. He wrote *Vegetable Kingdom* particularly for his daughters, to "show them the pleasure of a lifelong adventure with good, nourishing food." He thinks of himself "as a collagist—curating, cutting, pasting, and remixing staple ingredients, cooking techniques, and traditional Black dishes popular throughout the world to make [my] own signature recipes." Terry, who says the song "Beef" by Boogie Down Productions was one of the reasons he became vegan, pairs each recipe with a song, creating a tasty playlist.

Caramelized Leek and Seared Mushroom Toast with mustard pine nut spread, a dish in "Vegetable Kingdom" that Terry's younger daughter particularly loves

When Nadiya Hussain won the sixth season of *The Great British Bake Off*, she said "I'm never gonna put boundaries on myself ever again. I'm never gonna say I can't do it. I'm never gonna say 'maybe.' I'm never gonna say, 'I don't think I can.' I can and I will." Since then she has hosted nine television series and appeared on several others, and written five cookbooks, four children's books, three novels, and an autobiography.

One of the bakes that helped Hussein win "The Great British Bake Off" was a chocolate peacock.

In her cookbook *Cravings*, Chrissy Teigen writes, "Half the recipes in this book feel like they were developed by people with a bogus medical marijuana card." In 2019, she launched a website (cravingsbychrissyteigen.com) to complement her two cookbooks with additional easy recipes and behind-the-scenes looks at her family life with musician John Legend and their two children, plus guest appearances by Teigen's mother, Pepper.

Teigen says that her Spicy Miso Pasta recipe is the recipe everyone loves most.

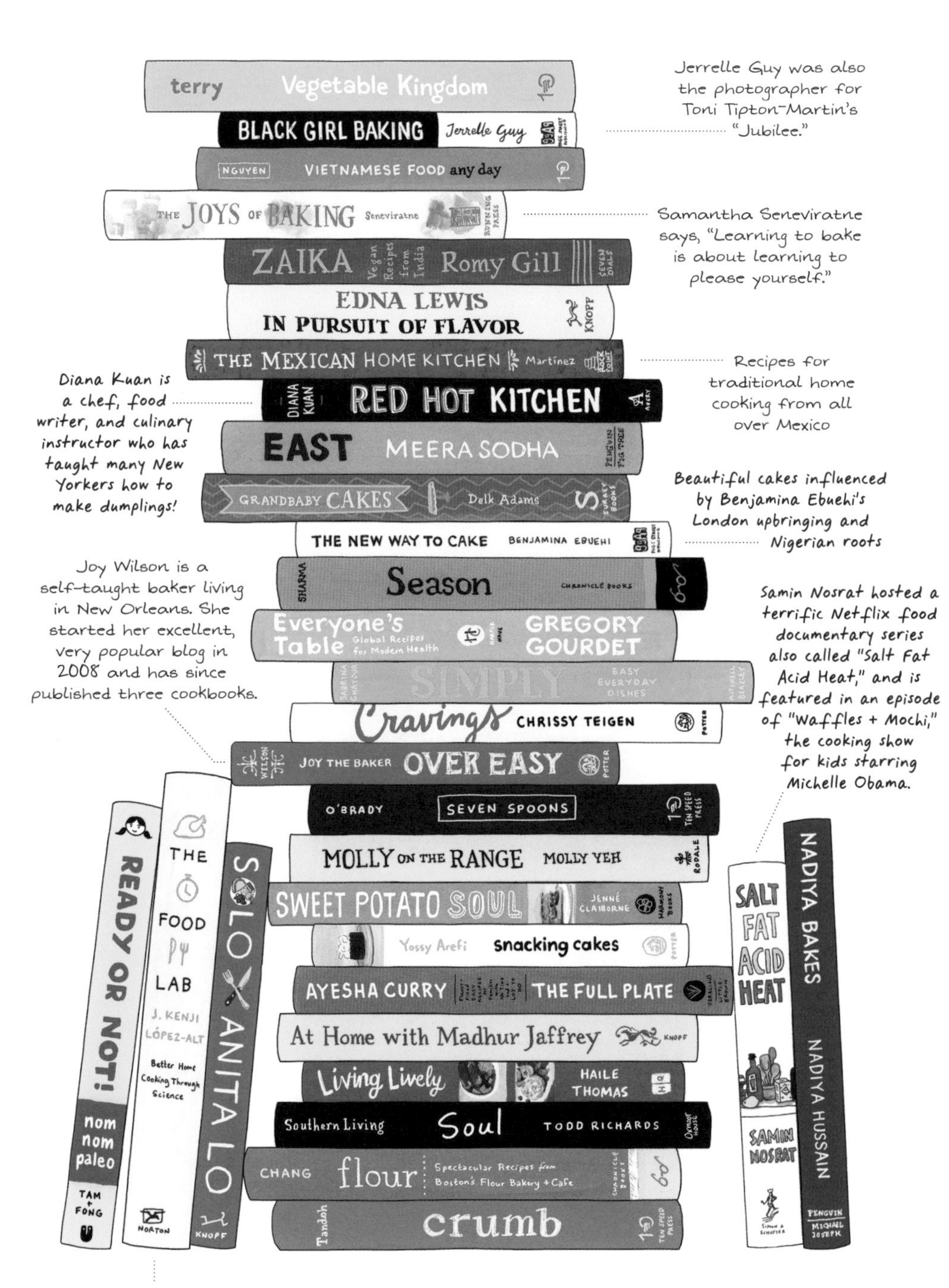
terry
Vegetable Kingdom
BLACK GIRL BAKING
Jerrelle Guy
NGUYEN
VIETNAMESE FOOD any day
THE JOYS OF BAKING
Seneviratne
ZAIKA
Vegan Recipes from India
Romy Gill
EDNA LEWIS
IN PURSUIT OF FLAVOR
KNOPF
THE MEXICAN HOME KITCHEN
Martinez
DIANA KUAN
RED HOT KITCHEN
AVERY
EAST
MEERA SODHA
GRANDBABY CAKES
Delk Adams
THE NEW WAY TO CAKE
BENJAMINA EBUEHI
SHARMA
Season
CHRONICLE BOOKS
Everyone's Table
Global Recipes for Modern Health
GREGORY GOURDET
SABRINA GHAYOUR
SIMPLY
EASY EVERYDAY DISHES
Cravings
CHRISSY TEIGEN
POTTER
WILSON
JOY THE BAKER
OVER EASY
POTTER
O'BRADY
SEVEN SPOONS
TEN SPEED PRESS
MOLLY ON THE RANGE
MOLLY YEH
RODALE
SWEET POTATO SOUL
JENNÉ CLAIBORNE
HARMONY BOOKS
Yossy Arefi
snacking cakes
POTTER
AYESHA CURRY
THE FULL PLATE
At Home with Madhur Jaffrey
KNOPF
Living Lively
HAILE THOMAS
Southern Living
Soul
TODD RICHARDS
OXMOOR HOUSE
CHANG
flour
Spectacular Recipes from Boston's Flour Bakery + Cafe
CHRONICLE BOOKS
Tandoh
crumb
TEN SPEED PRESS
READY OR NOT!
nom nom paleo
TAM + FONG
THE FOOD LAB
J. KENJI LÓPEZ-ALT
Better Home Cooking Through Science
NORTON
SOLO
ANITA LO
KNOPF
SALT FAT ACID HEAT
SAMIN NOSRAT
NADIYA BAKES
NADIYA HUSSAIN
PENGUIN
MICHAEL JOSEPH
Jerrelle Guy was also the photographer for Toni Tipton-Martin's "Jubilee."
Samantha Seneviratne says, "Learning to bake is about learning to please yourself."
Recipes for traditional home cooking from all over Mexico
Diana Kuan is a chef, food writer, and culinary instructor who has taught many New Yorkers how to make dumplings!
Beautiful cakes influenced by Benjamina Ebuehi's London upbringing and Nigerian roots
Joy Wilson is a self-taught baker living in New Orleans. She started her excellent, very popular blog in 2008 and has since published three cookbooks.
Samin Nosrat hosted a terrific Netflix food documentary series also called "Salt Fat Acid Heat," and is featured in an episode of "Waffles + Mochi," the cooking show for kids starring Michelle Obama.
J. Kenji López-Alt has done ALL the research.

WRITING ROOMS

NIK SHARMA

Author of *Season* and *The Flavor Equation*
Instagram/Twitter: @abrowntable

"My kitchen is the place where I not only cook meals for my family, but also where I develop and test recipes for work. While I did not design the current layout of the kitchen, it's provided me with a wonderful workspace. It's brightly lit, with views of my garden where I grow a lot of my ingredients that make it into my recipes. My kitchen's ambience is an important component of the energy that helps hone my vision of what I want to create and express in a meal."

Chronicle Books
2020 hardcover,
design by Lizzie Vaughan,
photo by Nik Sharma

Crown 2020 hardcover, photo by Nigel Livingstone

NIC STONE

Author of *Dear Martin* and *Dear Justyce*
Instagram: @nicstone / Twitter: @getnicced

"As a storyteller who understands the power and importance of setting on a character's narrative journey, the space where I dream up, ponder over, write down, and revise is vital to my journey as a storyteller. This was especially true in 2020 when that little ol' global pandemic known as the coronavirus forced all we fickle creatives to shelter—and create—in place. My home office was forced to evolve into a cozy daydream incubator, personal makerspace, reading room, and mini-museum of my favorite things (Marvel Funko Pops and LEGO BrickHeadz, anyone?). The dimpled bronze coffee table in front of the floor length mirror became the platform my computer sat on for Zoom events. The pink couch; gray, black, and white throw pillows; and trio of Chuck Styles paintings, my permanent virtual meeting and event background. And the more time I spent in it, the more okay I got with not being able to leave."

Known as one of the founders of the gourmet food truck movement, Roy Choi is the creator of the Korean Mexican taco truck Kogi.
Zoe's ghana Kitchen
ZOE ADJONYOH
MITCHELL BEAZLEY
L.A. SON
ROY CHOI
ALOHA KITCHEN
KYSAR
Alana Kysar grew up on Maui, and she gathered her favorite recipes from the islands.
Toni Tipton-Martin
Jubilee
POTTER
LARA LEE
COCONUT & SAMBAL
Lara Lee explored her heritage for this book, traveling around Indonesia and dining and learning in locals' homes.
LAZARUS LYNCH
SON of a SOUTHERN CHEF
AVERY
PONSECA
TRINIDAD
I AM A FILIPINO
ARTISAN
Culinary historian Michael W. Twitty traces the origins of Southern food.
THE COOKING GENE
A Journey Through African American Culinary History in the Old South
MICHAEL W. TWITTY
AMISTAD
Sherman
THE SIOUX CHEF'S INDIGENOUS KITCHEN
Priya Krishna's tribute to her mom Ritu's Indian American mashup cooking
Rose Water & Orange Blossoms
ABOOD
RUNNING PRESS
When on Maui, you must visit the two-time "Top Chef" finalist's take-out restaurant, Tin Roof! This cookbook features many of the classic dishes Simeon makes for his 'ohana.
Priya Krishna
INDIAN (-ish)
HMH
Esteban Castillo grew up in Santa Ana, California, and this book is full of Mexican food with American influences.
CHICANO EATS
ESTEBAN CASTILLO
JASON WANG
XI'AN FAMOUS FOODS
ABRAMS
Includes 150 recipes, each in honor of a Black chef, writer, or activist
MY SHANGHAI
Recipes and Stories from a City on the Water
BETTY LIU
To Asia, With Love
Hetty McKinnon
ZAITOUN
YASMIN KHAN
EVERYDAY and CELEBRATION
CARLA HALL'S SOUL FOOD
HARPER WAVE
SWEET HOME CAFE
COOKBOOK
A CELEBRATION OF AFRICAN AMERICAN COOKING
Smithsonian Books
THE AFRICA COOKBOOK
JESSICA B. HARRIS
New World SOURDOUGH
Bryan Ford
QUARRY
Hassan
In Bibi's Kitchen
HOONI KIM
WITH AKI KAMOZAWA
MY KOREA
TRADITIONAL FLAVORS, MODERN RECIPES
NORTON
Charles Phan
Vietnamese Home Cooking
TEN SPEED PRESS
BOTTOM of the POT
PERSIAN RECIPES AND STORIES
NAZ DERAVIAN
FLATIRON BOOKS
AGRAWAL
VIBRANT INDIA
JIKONI
RAVINDER BHOGAL
COOK REAL HAWAI'I
SHELDON SIMEON
WITH GARRETT SNYDER
POTTER
ALVIN CAILAN
AMBOY
HMH
BLACK COOKS AND THE SOUL OF AMERICAN FOOD
THE RISE
MARCUS SAMUELSSON
VORACIOUS
LITTLE, BROWN
Alvin Cailan is the Filipino creator of Eggslut in Los Angeles.

CELEBRATING IDENTITY THROUGH FOOD

Food is culture, and one of the most enjoyable ways to understand other people. The culinary traditions of marginalized groups have often been ignored, treated as inferior, eradicated, or even stolen. Some of these chefs and food writers aim to rediscover, reclaim, and revitalize traditional cuisines, while others explore how the food of their immigrant ancestors mashes up with the countries they now live in.

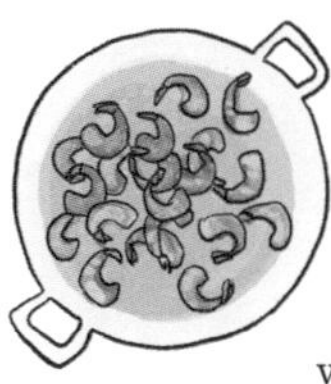

Louisiana Barbecued Shrimp, from "Jubilee"

For food journalist Toni Tipton-Martin's first book, *The Jemima Code*, she collected more than 150 Black-authored cookbooks, written over the course of two hundred years, and used them to tell the long-hidden history of Black cooking in America. For *Jubilee*, she gathered dishes from those, compared how they changed over the decades and from chef to chef, and included the ones with staying power. Tipton-Martin explains that unlike other immigrant groups well-known for their food in America, Black people "were brought here against our will and we were unable by law and threat of death to demonstrate any of our African-ness. . . . So while other cultures have come here and found mooring in their cultural food, we weren't able to do that."

The son of Honduran immigrants, Bryan Ford grew up in New York and New Orleans, and now lives in Miami. His book *New World Sourdough* reclaims the term, rescuing it from applying only to European-style boules. Most cultures around the world have traditions of naturally leavened bread, and Ford wants them to all be considered equally, and respected for how they achieve their intentions—to sandwich saucy fillings or be dunked in coffee, not just smeared with fresh butter and a sprinkling of fleur de sel. The recipes are down-to-earth and achievable, creating a much more inclusive vision of "artisan bread."

Ford grew up eating Honduran pan de coco from bodegas in New Orleans and includes a chocolate version in his book.

In an interview with Food52, the Oglala Lakota Sioux chef Sean Sherman said, "You think back on your ancestral lineage and the food that your grandparents and great-grandparents ate, and for a lot of Native communities across the United States and Canada, that food was forcibly and systematically taken away from these communities. We see the result of that with all these horrible health statistics." He and partner Dana Thompson founded the Sioux Chef, an organization dedicated to teaching others how to cook decolonized, unprocessed food, without things like sugar, dairy, and wheat flour.

Bison Pot Roast with Hominy

The bison population was decimated by white settlers throughout the 1800s, but has since made a comeback, and in this recipe, Sherman captures the traditional flavors of the Great Plains.

BOOKISH PEOPLE RECOMMEND

Balzer + Bray
2020 hardcover
design by Chris Kwon,
art by Alex Cabal

DR. TOYA SCAGGS

Organic chemist and bookstagrammer

Instagram:
@thereadingchemist
Twitter: @reading_chemist

Felix Ever After
by Kacen Callender

"Felix is Black, queer, and transgender. Felix has convinced himself that he's incapable of being loved because he's just one marginalization too many. This is a powerful coming-of-age story that focuses on love, acceptance, and self-discovery. There are so many reasons why this book is a must read (but we don't have time for that), so here are three reasons why you should read this book:

1) The normalized discussion of questioning one's gender identity even after the person has officially declared something. It is incredibly important for people to know that gender identity is fluid, and the author addresses this brilliantly.

2) The importance and necessity of more than romantic love (e.g. familial and friendship love) and how these types of love influence acceptance and self-discovery.

3) The discussion surrounding discrimination within the LGBTQIA+ community."

CARMEN ALVAREZ

Founder of Tomes & Textiles

Instagram:
@tomesandtextiles

Don't Date Rosa Santos
by Nina Moreno

Hyperion
2019 hardcover,
design by Mary
Claire Cruz, photo
by Michael Frost

"I wish I had this book as a teenager. In this contemporary novel, Rosa faces her family curse, tries to convince her grandmother to let her go to her college of choice, finds forbidden love, and deals with diaspora. Moreno weaves the complexities of the here-and-there Cuban heritage with a *Gilmore Girls* twist, balancing the relationships of three Cuban American women. It was a mirror into my childhood and my teen self would have appreciated seeing herself on the pages so, so much."

Harper
2019 hardcover,
design by Milan
Bozic

ZUBINA PATEL

Instagram:
@zubscovered

A Woman Is No Man
by Etaf Rum

"There is always this misconception, when reading books of this caliber, that at times the narrative has been overplayed in order to capture the hearts and thoughts of its readers. That perhaps the stories and ordeals suffered by those mentioned are in fact 'vamped' up to make the book more appealing. What if I told you that I am living proof of a daughter like Deya, and my mother is like Isra, who was subjected to the same treatments?"

ROXANNE GUZMÁN

Librarian

Instagram: @thenovelsanctuary

When I Was Puerto Rican
by Esmeralda Santiago

Vintage 1994 paperback, design by Megan Wilson, photo by Jack Delano

"Never has a book connected me more to home. Read and recommended to me by my mother, it allowed me to see and feel reflected in its pages the cool island breeze, the sweetness of a guava's nectar, the beauty and magic of the Puerto Rican youth."

Headline 2019 paperback, cover design and art by Richard Bravery

JERID P. WOODS

Co-host of *Books Are Pop Culture*

Instagram: @ablackmanreading

Parable of the Sower
by Octavia E. Butler

"Octavia Butler's *Parable of the Sower* demands that the reader analyze the way we interact with God through her characters. I took her challenge and vacillated between whether the Creator is a benevolent being or a clockmaker who set us in motion only to watch us tick. She reminds us that we are the sum of our experiences, and the trusted keepers of stories that matter to us from the Bible, Quran, the Bhagavad Gita, and countless other spiritual books. Her writing challenges the reader's comfort zone, and oftentimes closely resembles the mindscapes of those who travel within her pages."

REGGIE BAILEY

Co-host of *Books Are Pop Culture*

Instagram: @reggiereads

The Narrows
by Ann Petry

Mariner 2021 paperback, art by Nathan Burton

"This is one of the best novels you've never read. A literary masterpiece that fell to obscurity shortly upon its initial release in 1953 yet still holds a significant amount of weight when read in contemporary times. Its significance is maintained through Petry using an interracial love affair as an entry point to take on the topics of Black people and how their neighborhoods, lifestyles, and bodies are portrayed in the white media, through the harm caused on Black bodies via any accusations from whiteness, and the mental struggles that accompany the politics of respectability."

PERSONAL STORIES

The specifics in these memoirs are personal, but the circumstances are common, and the emotions are universal. We read memoirs to understand other people's lives, and to make sense of our own.

Roxane Gay has referred to her memoir *Hunger* as the book she "wanted to write the least," because of how honest she would need to be, and how much of herself she would need to expose. That led to the book being delayed a year as she procrastinated, she says, "because I was just dreading writing the book, while still feeling like this was a necessary book to write."

In *Ordinary Girls*, Jaquira Díaz tells how she grew up in an unstable home, with a drug-dealing father and a schizophrenic mother, leading her to rage and self-destructive behavior: fighting, using drugs, and even attempting suicide for the first time at age 11. On where she is now, as a successful writer, versus then, she told NPR's *Morning Edition* that "It felt like I was always, from the very beginning, trying to turn my life around, and it took a lot of people and a lot of stumbling and a lot of mistakes, until finally there were fewer mistakes."

Algonquin Books 2020 paperback, design by Adalis Martinez

Billy-Ray Belcourt dedicates his memoir-in-essays, *A History of My Brief Body,* "To those for whom utopia is a rallying call." When asked by the Rumpus for his idea of utopia, he said "I see bits and pieces of the utopian in the present: in how my people resist state violence and celebrate the joyousness of Indigenous life, in how queers and trans folks remake the codes of gender and embodiment, in how we love one another despite the injunction on care that capitalism implements."

Mariner Books 2015 paperback, design by Christopher Moisan

Fire Shut Up in My Bones is *New York Times* columnist Charles M. Blow's memoir about growing up in rural Louisiana and about being a victim of childhood sexual abuse. He started it when he was an art director at *National Geographic*, commuting from New York to Washington. "I hate to waste time, so I spent my time by writing about my life on the premise that I might be able to pitch those as short essays to magazines. It wasn't until later that I realized that I was writing a book."

Blow is an anchor for BNC news and often appears on CNN and MSNBC.

In his powerful memoir (which reads like a novel), Kiese Laymon shares the "heavy" weight of being a Black man in America.

A journey of self-discovery through an exploration of family history and DNA testing

Fifteen days after publication, Michelle Obama's memoir set the record as the highest-selling book published in the United States in 2018 with over two million copies sold.

A Black NYC man with little hiking experience decides to conquer the Appalachian trail.

Suleika Jaouad, diagnosed with leukemia at 22, struggles through long-term illness and finds herself on the other side.

About Jessica B. Harris's life in NYC in the 1970s, with friends like James Baldwin, Maya Angelou, Toni Morrison, and Nina Simone

Michelle Zauner is a songwriter and musician who performs as Japanese Breakfast.

BELOVED BOOKSTORES

MAHOGANYBOOKS

Washington, DC, USA
Instagram: @mahoganybooks

I was present at the virtual book club meeting for "A Promised Land", when author President Barack Obama surprised the group and joined the conversation.

MahoganyBooks was founded in 2007 by Derrick and Ramunda Young. This husband-and-wife duo is passionate about culture, community, and connection. Initially they operated solely online, making sure Black books were accessible and available to anyone wanting to read about Black culture. In 2017, they opened their first physical location in Anacostia, a historic neighborhood in Washington, DC, which had been without a bookstore for more than 20 years. Ramunda Young shares, "People come in here and say, 'Wow, I've been looking for books with my kids' faces on it' and to know that we can provide that . . . this helps with kids' self-esteem, identity, self-love." Operating in an area where 20% of middle schoolers read at their grade level, the Youngs also service local children through their give-back program, Books for the Block.

The bookstore is named after the Youngs' daughter, a 16-year-old entrepreneur who launched a handmade, eco-friendly candle company, the Green Things (@thegreen.things) in 2020.

BEL CANTO BOOKS

Long Beach, California, USA
Instagram: @belcantobooks

Bel Canto Books began as a monthly pop-up book club in 2017. Jhoanna Belfer, a Filipina American poet, left her corporate job as a hospitality executive to pursue her dream of opening an independent bookstore. In 2019, Belfer opened a brick-and-mortar space for Bel Canto Books in Long Beach, California. The store selections feature literary fiction, nonfiction, and children's books, celebrating women and people of color.

EPILOGUE BOOKS CHOCOLATE BREWS

Chapel Hill, North Carolina, USA
Instagram: @epiloguebooksch

Epilogue was founded in 2019 by husband-and-wife team Jaime and Miranda Sanchez, who met each other while working in retail. During a visit, you can browse an extensive book selection while enjoying coffee, churros, decadent chocolates, and besos, a sweet Mexican bread. The Sanchezes foster an atmosphere of inclusivity, and Jaime states that "we want to make sure stories told by women, minorities, [and] LGBTQ+ authors are the ones we amplify."

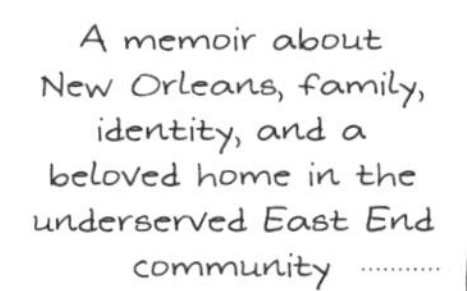

A compelling story about growing up in South Africa under apartheid and how being half-white and half-Black violated numerous laws

The memoir of Ojibwe writer Richard Wagamese, best known for his award-winning novel "Indian Horse"

A riveting story of hope and Brittany K. Barnett's commitment to transform the criminal justice system by winning freedom for people serving life sentences under outdated federal drug laws

MOORE
THE DRAGONS THE GIANT THE WOMEN
GRAYWOLF PRESS

CHILDREN OF THE LAND
MARCELO HERNANDEZ CASTILLO

BUI
THE BEST WE COULD DO
ABRAMS COMICARTS

More than 18 million people read Chanel Miller's victim impact statement, published by Buzzfeed in 2016.

The subtitle of this book is "A 6,000-Mile Marathon Through North America's Stolen Land."

The story of Anthony Ray Hinton, who spent 30 years on death row for a crime he did not commit

It sold over 1.7 million copies in its first week of release!

MACROCOSMIC MEMOIRS

Some memoirs are very intimate, while others use one person's true experiences to explore or explain a facet of the whole world. These are the latter.

Graywolf Press 2020 hardcover, design by Kimberly Glyder

The Dragons, the Giant, the Women is Wayétu Moore's memoir of her family's harrowing escape from Liberia during the civil war in 1989 that destroyed their comfortable life there. Her father (the "giant") kept them safe from the rebels (the "dragons"), while her mother returned from school at Columbia in New York to get them out, with the help of a young female soldier (the "women"). On what it's like to write a memoir, Moore notes, "the obvious restraint and fear and anxiety that . . . come[s] from creating characters out of people you know," and "how incredibly intimate it is to sort of dissect your own characteristics and habits in ways that you would a character in a novel."

In *Good Talk*, Mira Jacob uses drawings of herself and her family to illustrate their conversations, many of which are about the color of skin. She and her son are brown, and as he grows up in America, he has questions. It is heartbreaking at times, of course, but also very funny in parts. About that Jacobs said, "I'm a person that when I'm in pain I get kind of funnier and funnier. So the points in this where it's like laugh out loud funny, I know what's right under that."

One World 2019 hardcover, design by Rachel Ake

Carry is a memoir, but also a collection of well-researched essays on violence toward women and land, particularly Indigenous women and land, and gun violence. Toni Jensen does not, however, spend much of the book on mass shootings, because they actually make up only 1% of all shooting deaths in the United States. As she told *Shondaland*, "Most people who commit gun violence against you will be someone in your circle. Your father, your brother, your uncle, your coworker, your best friend's husband. It'll be one of those people."

Ballantine Books 2020 hardcover, design by Emily Mahon, art by Carmi Grau

"Qallunaat" is the Inuit word for people who are not Inuit, or in this case, the (mostly white) people living south of the Inuit community in James Bay in the Arctic, where Mini Aodla Freeman grew up. In 1957, she moved to Ottawa to be a translator for the Department of Aboriginal Affairs and Northern Development Canada, and *Life Among the Qallunaat* is Freeman's memoir of her life before, during, and after that change of setting.

University of Manitoba Press 2015 paperback, design by Mike Carroll, art by Elisapee Ishulutaq

INFLUENTIAL BOOK PEOPLE

WE NEED DIVERSE BOOKS

Instagram: @WeNeedDiverseBooks

We Need Diverse Books is a nonprofit and grassroots organization. Made up of children's book lovers, WNDB advocates for essential changes in the publishing industry to produce and promote literature that reflects and honors the lives of all young people.

"Children need to read books that reflect their own world, as well as learn about people whose worlds are very different from their own. Diverse books allow kids to have both—to see themselves reflected on the page for the first time, and to empathize with their neighbors, teachers, friends, and people around the globe. We Need Diverse Books started with the purpose of putting more diverse books into the hands of all kids, and we hope these selections will help you start to do that. Encourage the kids and teens in your life to read diverse books by diverse authors and to be intentional about their reading choices from a young age. Books shape our worldview and the beliefs we have about ourselves and the world around us. These books are just a starting place, and we encourage you to seek out diverse stories and authors whenever possible. Let's create a world where every child can see themselves in the pages of a book."

ETAF RUM

Creator of Books and Beans and author of *A Woman Is No Man*

Instagram: @booksandbeans

"While teaching college literature courses and noticing that most of the courses focused on white-centered experiences and narratives, I created Books and Beans on Instagram to give a voice to marginalized communities, especially women of color and stories focused on minorities. Our stories are often underrepresented in literature and Books and Beans was an attempt to counter this by highlighting the stories of people whose voices are often misrepresented, stereotyped, or silenced. This stack highlights some underrepresented communities and experiences by authors whose backgrounds are as diverse and rich as the stories they tell. I loved all of these books and I hope they resonate with readers."

"The books in this stack represent our dedication to amplifying the voices and stories of Black women, femmes, and nonbinary folks, not just in the United States but across the Black diaspora. As Audre Lorde said, "Black women are not one great vat of homogenized chocolate milk." Through fiction, nonfiction, and poetry, Black women from all over—Jamaica, the United States, Nigeria, London, Cameroon—tell their stories of joy, loss, kindness, hope, regret, of family, immigration, first love, and forgiveness. In this stack are stories about buying into the American dream, about finding language for mental health diagnoses, about the search for missing Black girls. These stories capture our collective grief and individual ways of moving through it, using beautiful language, innovative narrative structures, and so much heart."

GIZELLE FLETCHER

Founder of For Colored Girls Book Club

Instagram: @forcoloredgirlsbookclub

For Colored Girls Book Club was founded in Indianapolis, Indiana, in 2018 and is dedicated to amplifying the voices of Black and brown female and nonbinary writers in literature.

STUNNING GRAPHIC NOVELS

The term "graphic novel" refers to any standalone work in comics form (i.e., the narrative is mainly in pictures, and dialogue often in speech bubbles of some sort). So a book is often called a graphic novel even if it's a collection of short stories, nonfiction, or a memoir, and sometimes even if it's composed of serialized comic books collected into one volume. The gorgeous books shown here, many both written and illustrated by one person, cover all those categories.

Abrams ComicArts
2017 hardcover

KINDRED: A GRAPHIC NOVEL ADAPTATION

by Octavia E. Butler, adapted by Damian Duffy and John Jennings

Thirty-five-plus years after its original publication and 10+ years after Butler's death, Duffy and Jennings adapted this classic novel about a California woman's time travel back to the pre–Civil War South of her ancestors into a dynamic and gorgeous comic.

First Second
2017 paperback

PASHMINA

by Nidhi Chanani

Netflix is turning *Pashmina* into an animated musical, directed by Gurinder Chadha.

PERSEPOLIS

by Marjane Satrapi

One of the first graphic memoirs, this is Satrapi's account of her childhood in Iran during the Islamic Revolution.

Pantheon
2003 hardcover

THE PRINCE AND THE DRESSMAKER

by Jen Wang

A refreshing Cinderella-like story about teenage best friends in Paris and how some boys love to wear dresses and some girls love to create them.

First Second
2018 hardcover

HighWater Press
2019 paperback

THIS PLACE: 150 YEARS RETOLD

This anthology features 10 graphic stories told by Indigenous authors, all focused on the last 150 years of Canadian history, and a foreword by Alicia Elliott.

THIS ONE SUMMER

by Mariko Tamaki and Jillian Tamaki

Written by Mariko Tamaki and illustrated all in shades of blue by her cousin Jillian, it won the 2015 Eisner Award for Best New Graphic Novel.

First Second
2014 hardcover

BLACK PANTHER: A NATION UNDER OUR FEET

by Ta-Nehisi Coates and Brian Stelfreeze

Marvel Comics
2016 paperback

Coates, author of *Between the World and Me* and *We Were Eight Years in Power*, wrote a series of Black Panther comics for Marvel from 2016 to 2018.

I WAS THEIR AMERICAN DREAM

by Malaka Gharib

Clarkson Potter
2019 paperback

Another awesome memoir, this one is about coming of age as a Filipino Egyptian American.

AMERICAN BORN CHINESE

by Gene Luen Yang

First Second
2006 hardcover

Yang served as the U.S. National Ambassador for Young People's Literature from 2015 through 2016. Growing up he wanted to be a Disney animator until he discovered comic books.

THE ARRIVAL

by Shaun Tan

Arthur A. Levine Books
2007 hardcover

There are no words in here, just gorgeous images telling a story of the loneliness and hope of being an immigrant.

MARCH

by John Lewis, Andrew Aydin, and Nate Powell

Top Shelf Productions
2016 paperback slipcase set

An autobiographical trilogy about Congressman John Lewis's life in the Civil Rights Movement, *March: Book Three* won the 2016 National Book Award for Young People's Literature.

THE BEST WE COULD DO

by Thi Bui

Abrams
2017 hardcover

This heart-tugging memoir documents Bui's family's escape from war-torn Vietnam in the 1970s.

DISPLACEMENT

by Kiku Hughes

First Second
2020 hardcover

Hughes was inspired by *Kindred*, and here a Japanese American teen is pulled back in time to the U.S. concentration camp her grandmother was forced into during World War II.

NEW KID

by Jerry Craft

Quill Tree Books
2019 hardcover

This was the first graphic novel to win the Newbery Medal, in 2020!

HISTORY

As years go by, there appears to be less focus on the importance of knowing and remembering history. Lessons from the past, although they may not keep us from repeating the worst times, provide insight into the present and future. Unearthing forgotten stories is crucial in acknowledging the wealth of contributions by people of every background.

Congressman John Lewis described *March*, the first in a series, as a book "for all of America," and for young people, "to understand the essence of the Civil Rights Movement, to walk through the pages of history to learn about the philosophy and discipline of nonviolence, to be inspired to stand up to speak out and to find a way to get in the way when they see something that is not right, not fair, not just." Congressman Lewis was a champion for civil rights until the day he died on July 17, 2020.

The Great Migration (1916–1970) was the movement of six million African Americans relocating from the horrors of the South to cities in the North and West. This migration had a great impact on urban life and economic conditions in the United States. Isabel Wilkerson said she wanted to write *The Warmth of Other Suns* "because I felt it was this huge gap in American history, that it had such an effect on almost every aspect of our lives, from the music that we listen to, to the politics of our country, to the ways the cities even look and feel even today" and that "it was a forgotten chapter of history, and I wanted to elevate it in some ways to its rightful place in history."

This book should be required reading for all! A masterpiece!

Random House 2010 hardcover, design by Daniel Rembert

Top Shelf Productions 2019 paperback, art by Harmony Becker

In his graphic memoir, *They Called Us Enemy*, George Takei tells the story of his childhood spent in Japanese American internment camps. The attack on Pearl Harbor prompted President Roosevelt to sign an executive order that placed Japanese people, despite their American citizenship or length of residency, in detention centers. Although very young, Takei recalls, "I grew up as a child in American barbed wire prison camps." When asked why it is important to share this story he states, "our history is filled with a never-ending cycle of injustice, cruelty, and violence to minorities from the very beginning of our nation," and for this reason "I am hoping that there'll come a day when enough Americans know about this history—this dark and cruel history of America—that they will not allow it to repeat itself."

Clint Smith is also a poet and a staff writer at the Atlantic. This book looks at how different places in the U.S. deal with their history of slavery.

HOW THE WORD IS PASSED A RECKONING WITH THE HISTORY OF SLAVERY ACROSS AMERICA CLINT SMITH LITTLE, BROWN

Editors Ibram X. Kendi and Keisha N. Blain gather 90 brilliant writers to chronicle the four-hundred-year history (1619–2019) of Black America through essays, short stories, and personal reflections.

FOUR HUNDRED SOULS EDITED BY IBRAM X. KENDI AND KEISHA N. BLAIN ONE WORLD

PAUL ORTIZ AN AFRICAN AMERICAN AND LATINX HISTORY OF THE UNITED STATES BEACON PRESS

UNSEEN UNPUBLISHED BLACK HISTORY FROM THE NEW YORK TIMES PHOTO ARCHIVES BLACK DOG & LEVENTHAL PUBLISHERS

The incredible story of African American female mathematicians who played a vital role in NASA's space program

HIDDEN FIGURES MARGOT LEE SHETTERLY WM MORROW

Winner of the 2020 Caldecott Medal, this poetry picture book written by Kwame Alexander and illustrated by Kadir Nelson pays tribute to the struggles and triumphs of Black Americans past and present.

ALEXANDER NELSON THE UNDEFEATED VERSIFY

THE SWORD AND THE SHIELD THE REVOLUTIONARY LIVES OF MALCOLM X AND MARTIN LUTHER KING JR. PENIEL E. JOSEPH BASIC BOOKS

MARCH LEWIS AYDIN POWELL

A compilation about the people who migrated from different countries in Asia to the United States

The MAKING of ASIAN AMERICA ERIKA LEE SIMON & SCHUSTER

THE WARMTH OF OTHER SUNS ISABEL WILKERSON RANDOM HOUSE

NELSON HEART AND SOUL The Story of America and African Americans

a different mirror FOR YOUNG PEOPLE A History of Multicultural America Ronald Takaki

ILLUSTRATED BLACK HISTORY George McCalman AMISTAD

TAKEI THEY CALLED US ENEMY EISINGER · SCOTT · BECKER

THE GENE SIDDHARTHA MUKHERJEE SCRIBNER

ROXANNE DUNBAR-ORTIZ AN INDIGENOUS PEOPLES' HISTORY OF THE UNITED STATES BEACON PRESS

KILLING THE BLACK BODY DOROTHY ROBERTS VINTAGE

THIS PLACE: 150 Years Retold HWP

DAINA RAMEY BERRY AND KALI NICOLE GROSS A BLACK WOMEN'S HISTORY OF THE UNITED STATES BEACON PRESS

PHOTOGRAPHS BY JAMEL SHABAZZ BACK IN THE DAYS REMIX

STEPHANIE E. JONES-ROGERS THEY WERE HER PROPERTY Yale

NEVER CAUGHT ERICA ARMSTRONG DUNBAR

THE THREE MOTHERS ANNA MALAIKA TUBBS FLATIRON BOOKS

ARISING The DEAD ARE The Life of MALCOLM X LES PAYNE TAMARA PAYNE LIVERIGHT

A CHILD'S INTRODUCTION TO AFRICAN AMERICAN HISTORY JABARI ASIM Illustrated by LYNN GAINES

Queen Lili'uokalani was the last monarch of the Kingdom of Hawai'i, and this is her account of how the United States stole her land.

Liliuokalani HAWAII'S STORY BY HAWAII'S QUEEN Tuttle

A detailed account of contributions by Black women that impacted and transformed America

BOOKISH PEOPLE RECOMMEND

Katherine Tegen 2020 hardcover, art by Rachelle Baker

NNENNA ODELUGA

Bookstagrammer

Instagram/Twitter: @scsreads

Grown
by Tiffany D. Jackson

"This book was absolutely gripping and made my heart hurt. Some themes that Jackson writes about are the sexualization of Black girls, colorism, and racism. She points a light straight at the ugly truth: Black girls/women are constantly disrespected, neglected, and unprotected. I think the main message that Jackson was trying to convey is that we as a society need to protect Black girls, support them, and uplift them, because it's not easy to be a girl, and it's even more difficult to be a Black girl. This is a heavy read, but it's also an excellent and important one."

VICTORIA WOOD

Co-founder of BiblioLifestyle newsletter

Instagram: @bibliolifestyle

Augustown
by Kei Miller

Vintage 2017 paperback

"Each time I read it I discover something new. As Kei Miller writes, 'This is not another story about superstitious island people and their primitive beliefs.' We see how 'an event' is not the real story but the result of many others that have preceded it. The novel tells a community history from 1920 to 1982 and blends Jamaican folklore, oral storytelling traditions, and poetic prose. With vivid descriptions and memorable characters, I find myself thinking about them and their overlooked community long after I've turned the last page."

Dial 2016 hardcover, art by Kadir Nelson

RENÉE A. HICKS

Founder of Book Girl Magic

Instagram: @book_girl_magic
Twitter: @bookgirlmagic

Roll of Thunder, Hear My Cry
by Mildred D. Taylor

"When I think of my childhood and reading, Mildred D. Taylor is the first author that comes to mind. *Roll of Thunder, Hear My Cry* was a book that forever changed me. As a middle grade student, it was my first introduction to racism and how the lives of Black Americans (especially those living in the South) were greatly affected by it. It was also one of the first books I read that showed the strength, resilience, and togetherness of Black families when faced with life's tough obstacles. This book will forever be one that touches my soul and speaks to my heart."

GISSELLE DIAZ

Book blogger,
gissellereads.com

Instagram:
@gissellereads

Algonquin 2020 hardcover, art by Rachelle Baker

Furia
by Yamile Saied Méndez

"This is a great young adult book! Furia tells the story of Camila, a young girl in Rosario, Argentina, who wants to pursue her dream of playing professional soccer in a world where there's no place for the ambition for a girl. It is full of character development and in a great setting. You'll be transported to Rosario and fall in love with Camila. She is a young woman who rises above societal expectations and carves her own path. This is a powerful novel that will stay with me for a while."

BUFFY HOLMES

Founder of Queens Literary Collective Book Club

Instagram: @msbszenlife

Virago 1986 paperback

Their Eyes Were Watching God
by Zora Neale Hurston

"This gem of the Harlem Renaissance is set in the late 1920s and centers around the Black town of Eatonville, Florida. Rich in language and the use of Black dialect written exactly as it is spoken, this book was like none I had ever read before. It felt real, it felt authentic, and it felt like home. It is a story of women's empowerment and self-realization that embodies everything that was Zora Neale Hurston. It resonates with me because as a Black woman, I have not only endured situations where I was placed in a box, silenced, and expected to do what others wanted me to do, I have seen this play out generation after generation with Black women who give everything and simply want love in return. Janie and Zora both decided to live life on their own terms and the strength in their stories inspire. Every time I read it, I find a little bit more of myself."

SOL KELLY

Graduate student and bookstagrammer

Instagram: @thesolreader

Harper Perennial 2007 paperback, design by Mary Schuck, photo by Jan Cobb

The Collected Poetry of Nikki Giovanni
by Nikki Giovanni

"Nikki Giovanni is one of the most renowned Black poets, and her poems reflect Black power and excellence, family and friends, love, memories, life, and more. *The Collected Poetry of Nikki Giovanni* is a treasure for all poetry lovers to cherish. Inside you will find a collection of her early work from 1968 to 1998: *Black Feeling Black Talk, Black Judgement, Re: Creation, My House, The Women and the Men, Cotton Candy on a Rainy Day,* and *Those Who Ride the Night Winds*, as well as timeless and sentimental pieces such as *Ego Tripping* and *Resignation*. In this collection we witness how Giovanni grows and elevates as a poet, as she gives us insight into her life and emotions and her perspective on the world around her."

WRITING ROOMS

EDDIE S. GLAUDE JR.

Author of *Begin Again*
Instagram/Twitter: @esglaude

"My writing space is cluttered. Books and papers surround me like companions who whisper thoughts in my ear. It looks a mess, but it has some semblance of order. I know where the things that matter are. Every time I reach for a book or search through a stack of papers, I am reminded of the grand tradition that inspires me. When my son was younger—he has since left home—he described my writing space as a cave, especially when I was in the throes of a book project. I would disappear for hours on end. I still do."

Crown 2020 hardcover, design by Michael Morris, photo by Kathleen Pakay/ Hudson Film Works II

Catapult
2018 hardcover,
design by Donna Cheng

NICOLE CHUNG

Author of *All You Can Ever Know*
Instagram/Twitter: @nicolesjchung

"Having my own writing space is relatively new for me. My husband, kids, and I have lived in our house for about two years. Before that, we moved three times in seven years, so I never felt quite 'settled' enough to get attached to certain spaces—I wrote *All You Can Ever Know* in a variety of spots, from my standing desk to our kitchen table to this comfy old blue couch I'll never get rid of. But when we moved into our current place, we had an extra bedroom for the first time since before kids—10' x 10' or thereabouts, the smallest room in the house that's not a bathroom—and I immediately snagged it for my own.

Having this space feels good, first and foremost, because it's a room of my own with a door that I can close—something I haven't had since I was a kid. I love having a reserved space for my work.

But to tell the truth, it took weeks for me to learn to write here, because I'd never really had a dedicated working/writing space before. Such luxury! So much pressure! The first time I sat down to write at the desk, I thought, if you can't write and produce work you're proud of here, in this comfortable, undisturbed little room with sunlight streaming in through the window and a lock on the door, what kind of writer are you?

In every other room, others (rightly) have some claim to me, my labor, my time. This space was set up to be a kind of retreat, a writing retreat, right in my own home."

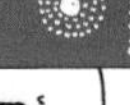

TA-NEHISI COATES

THE TRUTHS WE HOLD
KAMALA HARRIS

Kamala Harris made history when she became the United States' first woman, first Black, and first Asian American vice president and the highest-ranking female elected official in U.S. history.

Rez Life DAVID TREUER

DEAR AMERICA, Notes of an Undocumented Citizen Jose Antonio Vargas

BLACK MAGIC

BEGIN AGAIN EDDIE S. GLAUDE JR.

AMERICAN HARVEST ✦ MARIE MUTSUKI MOCKETT

Marie Mutsuki Mockett, raised in California, explores the rural American heartland after inheriting a Nebraska wheat farm and learns much about people.

FINDING LATINX PAOLA RAMOS

An exploration of what it means to be Latinx in the United States

STAMPED FROM THE BEGINNING The Definitive History of Racist Ideas in America — Ibram X. Kendi

When this won the National Book Award for Nonfiction in 2016, Ibram X. Kendi became the youngest writer to win that award, and in his speech, he paid tribute to "the human beauty in the resistance to racism."

FROM A NATIVE DAUGHTER HAUNANI-KAY TRASK

A TERRIBLE THING TO WASTE ENVIRONMENTAL RACISM AND ITS ASSAULT ON THE AMERICAN MIND HARRIET A. WASHINGTON

BLACK FUTURES KIMBERLY DREW + JENNA WORTHAM

Karla Cornejo Villavicencio The Undocumented Americans

My Vanishing Country Bakari Sellars

BLACK FATIGUE MARY-FRANCES WINTERS

Mary-Frances Winters, a diversity and inclusion expert, coined the term "Black fatigue" for the impact of systemic racism on Black people in corporate spaces.

IT'S NOT ABOUT THE BURQA EDITED BY MARIAM KHAN

EVE L. EWING GHOSTS IN THE SCHOOLYARD

STACEY ABRAMS OUR TIME IS NOW

How the Other Half Banks BARADARAN

Atul Gawande Being Mortal

DIVERSITY, INC. PAMELA NEWKIRK

The Ungrateful Refugee Dina Nayeri

DAYNA BOWEN MATTHEW JUST MEDICINE A CURE FOR RACIAL INEQUALITY IN AMERICAN HEALTHCARE

Wes Moore THE WORK

THE DEVIL'S HIGHWAY LUIS ALBERTO URREA

RACELESS IN SEARCH OF FAMILY, IDENTITY, AND THE TRUTH ABOUT WHERE I BELONG GEORGINA LAWTON

SIMPSON AS WE HAVE ALWAYS DONE

Disability Visibility EDITED BY Alice Wong

DINA GILIO-WHITAKER AS LONG AS GRASS GROWS THE INDIGENOUS FIGHT FOR ENVIRONMENTAL JUSTICE, FROM COLONIZATION TO STANDING ROCK

Ijeoma Oluo MEDIOCRE The Dangerous Legacy of White Male America

edited by CINELLE BARNES A MEASURE OF BELONGING

EXAMINING SOCIETY

A true examination of society is not revealed through one group, but by delving into the many cultures that make up our diverse world. These stories help you cross boundaries, foster persistent social interaction, and gain awareness to connect to a world outside of your own.

One World 2020 hardcover, design by Greg Mollica

Co-editors Kimberly Drew and Jenna Wortham share in the introduction that "in developing *Black Futures,* we sought to answer the question: What does it mean to be Black and alive right now?" The book is a collection of Black life in photographs, essays, poems, narratives, interviews and more. They reveal that the Black Futures Project "started a few years ago as a direct message exchange on Twitter and has evolved into a shared desire to archive a moment" and it is not a linear work: "like us, this book lives and breathes beyond temporal Western frameworks."

Stacey Abrams's *Our Time Is Now: Power, Purpose, and the Fight for a Fair America* is a manifesto, a call to the "New American Majority—that coalition of people of color, young people and moderate to progressive whites." Abrams ran for governor of Georgia in 2018, winning the hearts and minds of many. In 2019, she founded Fair Fight to advocate for fair elections and battle voter suppression. She works tirelessly for change and that change happens, such as when two Democrats (Rev. Raphael Warnock and Jon Ossoff) won Georgia's Senate seats in a 2021 election run-off. When asked about the book's title, she said, "This is a nation that is more diverse than it has ever been. This is a nation that has seen the consequences of conservative behavior. And now people know they can do something about it."

Vintage 2020 paperback, design by Madeline Partner

Diagnosed with spinal muscular dystrophy as a baby, Alice Wong is a fierce advocate and activist for disability rights. As the editor of *Disability Visibility*, Wong stated that "this book is a snapshot of what the disabled experience is like for some people." She was recognized by President Obama during the 25th Anniversary of the Americans with Disabilities Act (ADA). Although Wong could not attend in person, she met the president via a telepresence robot that showed her face on a computer screen, and she controlled the robot's movements from her home computer.

Wong appeared at the White House via a Beam Pro telepresence robot!

READ AROUND THE WORLD

Books inspired by the author's connection to that country.

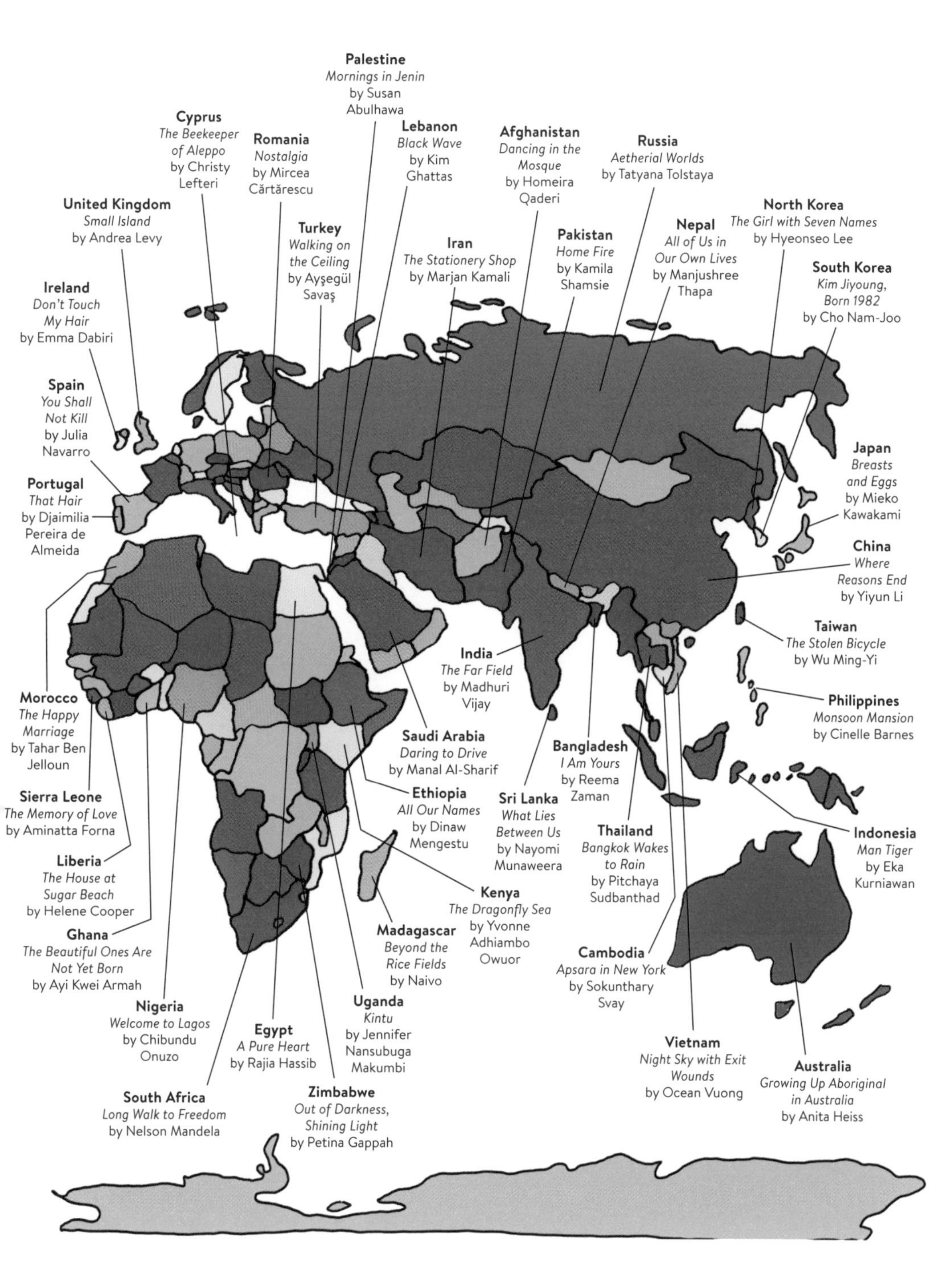
Palestine
Mornings in Jenin
by Susan Abulhawa
Cyprus
The Beekeeper of Aleppo
by Christy Lefteri
Romania
Nostalgia
by Mircea Cărtărescu
Lebanon
Black Wave
by Kim Ghattas
Afghanistan
Dancing in the Mosque
by Homeira Qaderi
Russia
Aetherial Worlds
by Tatyana Tolstaya
United Kingdom
Small Island
by Andrea Levy
Turkey
Walking on the Ceiling
by Ayşegül Savaş
Iran
The Stationery Shop
by Marjan Kamali
Pakistan
Home Fire
by Kamila Shamsie
Nepal
All of Us in Our Own Lives
by Manjushree Thapa
North Korea
The Girl with Seven Names
by Hyeonseo Lee
South Korea
Kim Jiyoung, Born 1982
by Cho Nam-Joo
Ireland
Don't Touch My Hair
by Emma Dabiri
Spain
You Shall Not Kill
by Julia Navarro
Japan
Breasts and Eggs
by Mieko Kawakami
Portugal
That Hair
by Djaimilia Pereira de Almeida
China
Where Reasons End
by Yiyun Li
Taiwan
The Stolen Bicycle
by Wu Ming-Yi
India
The Far Field
by Madhuri Vijay
Morocco
The Happy Marriage
by Tahar Ben Jelloun
Philippines
Monsoon Mansion
by Cinelle Barnes
Saudi Arabia
Daring to Drive
by Manal Al-Sharif
Bangladesh
I Am Yours
by Reema Zaman
Sierra Leone
The Memory of Love
by Aminatta Forna
Ethiopia
All Our Names
by Dinaw Mengestu
Sri Lanka
What Lies Between Us
by Nayomi Munaweera
Thailand
Bangkok Wakes to Rain
by Pitchaya Sudbanthad
Indonesia
Man Tiger
by Eka Kurniawan
Liberia
The House at Sugar Beach
by Helene Cooper
Kenya
The Dragonfly Sea
by Yvonne Adhiambo Owuor
Ghana
The Beautiful Ones Are Not Yet Born
by Ayi Kwei Armah
Madagascar
Beyond the Rice Fields
by Naivo
Cambodia
Apsara in New York
by Sokunthary Svay
Nigeria
Welcome to Lagos
by Chibundu Onuzo
Uganda
Kintu
by Jennifer Nansubuga Makumbi
Egypt
A Pure Heart
by Rajia Hassib
Vietnam
Night Sky with Exit Wounds
by Ocean Vuong
Australia
Growing Up Aboriginal in Australia
by Anita Heiss
South Africa
Long Walk to Freedom
by Nelson Mandela
Zimbabwe
Out of Darkness, Shining Light
by Petina Gappah

EDITIONS

Gabriel García Márquez's *One Hundred Years of Solitude* was first published by Editorial Sudamericana in 1967, in Spanish, as *Cien años de soledad*. García Márquez first sat down to write it in the summer of 1965 and then "did not get up for eighteen months," crafting the novel that would first inspire the term "magical realism" while smoking over 30,000 cigarettes. Much-loved from the get-go, the story of the Buendía family of Macondo, a fictional city in Colombia, has since been translated into more than 40 languages and has sold over 50 million copies, and helped García Márquez win the Nobel Prize in Literature in 1982. Here are the covers of several different editions, from countries all over the world.

ARGENTINA

Editorial Sudamericana 1967 paperback, design by Iris Pagano

García Márquez's friend Vicente Rojo was hired to design the first edition cover, but when he didn't turn in the art in time, in-house designer Pagano created this for the initial print run.

ARGENTINA

Editorial Sudamericana 1967 paperback, design by Vicente Rojo

Mexican painter Rojo's design was used for the second edition, released the same year. This is the cover seen in the famous photo of García Márquez wearing the book on his head.

UNITED KINGDOM

Jonathan Cape 1970 hardcover, design by Toni Evora

This is the first UK edition!

UNITED STATES

Harper & Row 1975 hardcover, design by Guy Fleming

This was the first U.S. edition!

BULGARIA

Отечествения фронт 1971 hardcover

SERBIA

BIGZ 1976
paperback

BRAZIL

José Olympio
Editora 1985
paperback

UNITED KINGDOM

Penguin Books
1999 paperback, art
by Támas Galambos

← This cover features the right half of Galambos's 1981 painting "Summer," and those hills are actually the bent legs of a reclining female figure.

JAPAN

Shinchōsha
2006 paperback

SWEDEN

Wahlström
& Widstrand
2012 hardcover

UNITED STATES

Barnes & Noble
2011 hardcover,
art by
Cathie Bleck

ESTONIA

Eesti Raamat
2017 hardcover

← The novel turned 50 years old in 2017, so many new editions were released that year.

SPAIN

Penguin Random
House Grupo
Editorial
2017 hardcover,
art by
Luisa Rivera

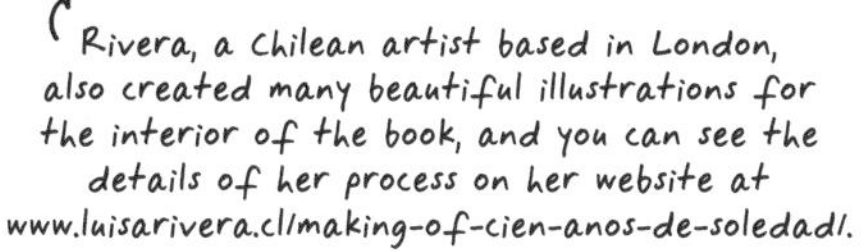
Rivera, a Chilean artist based in London, also created many beautiful illustrations for the interior of the book, and you can see the details of her process on her website at www.luisarivera.cl/making-of-cien-anos-de-soledad/.

SLOVAKIA

Slovart 2017
hardcover

ANTIRACIST READING

These are all great, informative books. You should read them and sit with the knowledge you've gained until it becomes part of you. And *then*, you should go out and actively work to help create a society that no longer believes in white supremacy.

Ibram X. Kendi is the founding director of the Antiracist Research and Policy Center at American University, and he says it's not enough to "not be racist"; that in fact there is no such state. You are either actively antiracist, or you're racist, but neither is permanent. To be antiracist, you must first see all the racial groups as equal, and you must realize that any inequality is a result of racist policies, not a group's inferiority. And then you must figure out what policies you are most passionate about reforming, and actively work to do that, by donating time or money. "Fundamentally," he believes, "an antiracist is a part of the struggle that is challenging racism on an everyday basis."

Heather McGhee uses economic data to show "that discriminatory laws and practices that target African Americans also negatively impact society at large," making the case that everyone would benefit from "progress for people of color," including white people. Her three-year journey in writing *The Sum of Us* took from her home in New York City to California, Mississippi, Maine, and other states. McGhee "tried to include stories of people who are living in the America we want for everyone," adding that "I want people to see the world we might have."

McGhee wanted her book cover to "look more like a book of literary fiction than a book about the economy."

One World 2021 hardcover, design by Rachel Ake, art by David McConochie

One World 2020 hardcover, design by Na Kim

Cathy Park Hong wrote *Minor Feelings* to explain what it's like not being white in a country where belonging means being white. By "minor feelings" she means sustained, negative emotions caused by racial microaggressions and the gaslighting that comes with them, "the irritant of having one's perception of reality constantly questioned or dismissed." They are feelings you're stuck with, the ongoing "trauma of living in a racist, capitalist society."

Austin Channing Brown's *I'm Still Here* is an account of her life surrounded by white people in schools and churches, and how she learned "to love Blackness," and how we can create a society that's truly inclusive instead of just pretending while it's trendy to do so. She wrote the book particularly for women of color, "So that the next time you have a white person who is like, 'Can you help me?' all you have to do is whip out this book and slide it across the table and be like, 'Yup, read that.'"

Convergent Books 2018 hardcover, design by Na Kim

The Fire Next Time James Baldwin
Dial
Just Mercy Bryan Stevenson
Spiegel & Grau
Desmond Cole The Skin We're In
when they call you a terrorist
a black lives matter memoir
patrisse khan-cullors & asha bandele
Ta-Nehisi Coates | Between the World and Me
Michelle Alexander The New Jim Crow
me and white supremacy Saad
The Devil You Know A Black Power Manifesto Charles M. Blow
Inventing Latinos
Jason Reynolds Ibram X. Kendi Stamped Racism, Antiracism, and You
Little, Brown
How We Fight White Supremacy Akiba Solomon and Kenrya Rankin
Minor Feelings Cathy Park Hong
One World
How to Be an Antiracist Ibram X. Kendi
part asian · 100% hapa portraits by kip fulbeck
Why I'm No Longer Talking to White People About Race Reni Eddo-Lodge
Just Us Claudia Rankine
I'm Still Here Austin Channing Brown
Convergent
Alicia Garza The Purpose of Power
The Fire This Time Jesmyn Ward
Moustafa Bayoumi How Does It Feel to Be a Problem? Being Young and Arab in America
Carol Anderson, Ph.D. White Rage The Unspoken Truth of Our Racial Divide
Tatum Why Are All the Black Kids Sitting Together in the Cafeteria?
Basic Books
So you want to talk about race Ijeoma Oluo
Seal Press
Michael Eric Dyson Tears We Cannot Stop
St. Martin's Press
Isabel Wilkerson Caste
Random House
Bringing Up Race Uju Asika
Yellow Kite
America for Americans A History of Xenophobia in the United States Lee
Basic Books
This Book Is Anti-Racist Tiffany Jewell
FL
The Sum of Us Heather McGhee
One World
Coates's book, a letter to his teenage son, won the 2015 National Book Award for Nonfiction, and Toni Morrison called it "required reading." What more do you need to know?
Bryan Stevenson is the founder of the Equal Justice Initiative, which is "committed to ending mass incarceration and excessive punishment in the U.S., challenging racial and economic injustice, and protecting basic human rights for the most vulnerable people in American society."
Michelle Alexander is a lawyer and civil-rights advocate.
Laura E. Gómez explains "how and why Latinos became cognizable as a racial group" in the United States.
The newest edition of this book includes an afterword on how the coronavirus pandemic has "turbocharged" xenophobia in America.
An excellent starting point, especially for teens
An actionable guidebook on how to have honest conversations about race and how to do the work to dismantle the racial divide

BELOVED BOOKSTORES

SOURCE BOOKSELLERS

Detroit, Michigan, USA
Instagram: @sourcebooksellers

Janet Webster Jones, a retired educator who spent 40 years in the Detroit Public School system, has been a bookseller since 1989. In 2002, she opened her first brick-and-mortar store, Source Booksellers, in Detroit's midtown area and in 2013, moved to their current home in the new Auburn Building. Janet has always had a love for books. The daughter of a librarian, she recalls frequent trips to her neighborhood's Detroit Public Library branch. Source Booksellers hosts a unique niche of nonfiction books. The store curates text on history and culture, health and well-being, metaphysics and spirituality, and books by and about women. They welcome the community and visitors to join them for weekly events, which include author talks, poetry readings, community conversations, and a free Saturday morning exercise class.

IRON DOG BOOKS

Vancouver, British Columbia, Canada
Instagram: @irondogbooks

Iron Dog Books is an Indigenous-owned bookshop and booktruck that began as a mobile bookshop in an 80-square-foot van—how cool is that?! Husband and wife owners, Hilary and Cliff Atelo, believe that books should be affordable and accessible, and for two years the booktruck rolled to wherever readers were located. In 2019, Iron Dog Books found a permanent home in the Hastings-Sunrise neighborhood of Vancouver. Readers can now find new, used, and remaindered books as well as other merchandise, in a warm inviting atmosphere. When asked what author they would most like to host for an event, owners Hilary and Cliff, both fans of feminist science fiction and fantasy, agreed that they would love to have N. K. Jemisin visit their shop. The bookstore allows customers to bring in second-hand books for store credit to be used for anything in the store, or they can donate their store credit to local organizations in need.

HARRIETT'S BOOKSHOP

Philadelphia, Pennsylvania, USA
Instagram: @harrietts_bookshop

Named for historical heroine Harriet Tubman, Harriett's Bookshop highlights women authors, women artists, and women activists. In 2020, Jeannine Cook opened Harriett's Bookshop in Philadelphia's Fishtown neighborhood, a majority white neighborhood with a history of high racial tension. Cook opened the space "for folks to come together, discuss ideas, and debate in a healthy way." Harriett's hosts writers' groups, small concerts, and group discussions on community-building. Cook, a former educator, says, "If people want to educate themselves, then I want to fill that gap, making sure they get that information. There's no greater joy in my life."

On many occasions you can find Cook and her team passing out free books outside the shop on Girard Avenue and in other places around the city.

Moraga & Anzaldúa This Bridge Called My Back Fourth Edition SUNY
Shen Bad Girls Throughout History CHRONICLE BOOKS
PILLOTON GIRLS GARAGE chronicle books
Established in 2013, Girls Garage is a nonprofit design and building program and dedicated workspace for girls ages 9–18.
CROSSFIRE STACEYANN CHIN
MOHANTY FEMINISM WITHOUT BORDERS DUKE
VASHTI HARRISON Little Leaders BOLD WOMEN IN BLACK HISTORY
Highlighting the contributions of 40 African American women who impacted history
I Am Malala MALALA YOUSAFZAI
In 2015, the Swedish government gave a copy of this book to every 16-year-old in the country.
MIKKI KENDALL HOOD FEMINISM VIKING
WE SHOULD ALL BE FEMINISTS CHIMAMANDA NGOZI ADICHIE ANCHOR BOOKS
THIS WILL BE MY UNDOING MORGAN JERKINS HARPER PERENNIAL
Roxane Gay believes "it is better to be a bad feminist than no feminist."
HOW WE GET FREE EDITED BY KEEANGA-YAMAHTTA TAYLOR
Bad Feminist Essays Roxane Gay HARPER PERENNIAL
These essays center Black womanhood and Brittney Cooper's passion for Black women and girls.
Maxine Hong Kingston The Woman Warrior
feminism is for everybody bell hooks Routledge
CHARLENE A. CARRUTHERS UNAPOLOGETIC A BLACK, QUEER, AND FEMINIST MANDATE FOR RADICAL MOVEMENTS BEACON PRESS
An examination of the feminist movement in the United States, focusing on the intersections of gender, race, and class
ELOQUENT RAGE BRITTNEY COOPER ST. MARTIN'S PRESS
Clarissa Pinkola Estés, Ph.D. Women Who Run With the Wolves Myths and Stories of the Wild Woman Archetype
WHITE TEARS / BROWN SCARS RUBY HAMAD Catapult
NEW EDITION COLONIZE THIS! EDITED BY DAISY HERNÁNDEZ & BUSHRA REHMAN SEAL
SARA AHMED Living a Feminist Life DUKE
FEMINISTA JONES RECLAIMING OUR SPACE BEACON PRESS
Melissa V. Harris-Perry Sister Citizen Yale
WAYWARD LIVES, BEAUTIFUL EXPERIMENTS INTIMATE HISTORIES OF SOCIAL UPHEAVAL SAIDYA HARTMAN NORTON
PENGUIN VITAE SISTER OUTSIDER AUDRE LORDE
ANGELA Y. DAVIS WOMEN, RACE & CLASS VINTAGE
Set a record, spending 145 weeks on the "New York Times" best-seller list

FEMINISM

To bring about social change, solidarity cannot be a one-way street. For many years mainstream feminism has overlooked and excluded Black women and women of color. As bell hooks eloquently states in her book *Feminism is for Everybody: Passionate Politics,* "As long as women are using class or race power to dominate other women, feminist sisterhood cannot be fully realized."

Catapult 2020 paperback, design by Na Kim

Ruby Hamad reads one book at a time and has no reservations about giving up on a book a few chapters in. In 2018, Ruby Hamad's *Guardian* article, "How white women use strategic tears to silence women of colour," went viral and generated more than 125,000 shares across the world. This article was the catalyst for her debut book, *White Tears/Brown Scars: How White Feminism Betrays Women of Color.*

Viking 2020 hardcover, design by Lynn Buckley

When asked what "hood feminism" is, activist Mikki Kendall replied that it is the "actual lived feminist experience of helping others get access to their basic needs." Kendall, a veteran of the U.S. Army, left her government job at the Department of Veterans Affairs in 2013 to pursue her writing career full-time. Kendall believes we should lift up all women and that "for this freedom, this liberation we are striving towards, we have to be willing to reach back and help the folks who face the most obstacles."

Knopf 1976 hardcover, design by Lidia Ferrara, art by Elias Dominguez

Winner of the 1976 National Book Critics Circle Award for Nonfiction, *The Woman Warrior* by Maxine Hong Kingston mixes memoir with Chinese folktales. The book is divided into five parts and reads like short stories. Kingston reflects on growing up as the child of immigrant parents and dealing with sexism and racism in her new land and her parents' old one.

Persephone Press 1981 hardcover, art by Johnetta Tinker, design by Maria von Brincken

This Bridge Called My Back: Writings by Radical Women of Color, a 1981 feminist classic, was updated and re-released in 2015 in response to a new generation of young activists fighting for inclusion and social change. The anthology has influenced women of color for decades and it explores, as Cherríe Moraga puts it, "the complex confluence of identities—race, class, gender, and sexuality—systemic to women of color oppression and liberation."

AUTHORS RECOMMEND

TAYARI JONES

Author of *An American Marriage* and *Silver Sparrow*

Instagram/Twitter: @tayari

Meridian
by Alice Walker

Open Road Media e-book, design and art by Kimberly Glyder

"Of all of Alice Walker's novels, *Meridian* is my favorite. It's one of those books that I read when I was about 18 or 19 and I just didn't quite get it. My professor at Spelman was standing in the front of the class, swooning and moved almost to tears, and I was just sort of confused. I revisited it as a grown woman and was awestruck by the story, the writing, the characters, and the WISDOM.

Set during the Civil Rights Movement, this is a novel that reminds you that freedom begins at home. At the heart are three seekers—Meridian, a Black woman; Truman, a Black man; and Lynne, a white woman. It's a love triangle that is about more than just sex. Walker confronts the Big Ideas about the human condition and manages to leave the reader shaken and inspired at the same time."

CATHERINE ADEL WEST

Author of *Saving Ruby King*

Instagram/Twitter: @cawest329

Kindred
by Octavia E. Butler

Headline 2018 UK paperback, design and art by Yeti Lambregts

"When Black women are no longer agents of our bodies; when our control is stolen and we must make do with the inequitable, racist, and abhorrent world surrounding us, who do we become? How can we reconcile with those who oppress us, but are still for better or worse, our blood family? The best thing about *Kindred* is that while quietly drawing you into its world, the book deals with these unsettling questions and there are no objective answers. This makes it life-altering, and I savored every word I could. Octavia Butler created an iconic story still reverberating throughout the literary pantheon."

NGUYỄN PHAN QUẾ MAI

Author of *The Mountains Sing*

Instagram: @nguyenphanquemai_
Twitter: @nguyen_p_quemai

Grove Press 2015 hardcover, design and art by Christopher Moisan

The Sympathizer
by Viet Thanh Nguyen

"I read to be entertained, to be educated, and to be challenged. For those reasons, I highly recommend *The Sympathizer* by Viet Thanh Nguyen. The novel is narrated by a nameless character who calls himself 'a spy, a sleeper, a spook, a man of two faces.' Highly intelligent and humorous, this novel puts Vietnamese people on equal level with Americans. It criticizes all sides of the Vietnam War, and it challenges the readers' privileges and assumptions. The book made me laugh out loud one moment and weep the next. Its poetic prose and insightful observations of the human characters demand me to savor it again and again."

NATALIA SYLVESTER

Author of *Everyone Knows You Go Home* and *Running*

Instagram/Twitter:
@nataliasylv

One World 2020 hardcover, design by Rachel Ake

The Undocumented Americans
by Karla Cornejo Villavicencio

"At a time when reading is seen as a tool of empathy (but seldom, action) and the stories of marginalized people are often consumed by a white gaze to 'teach,' Karla Cornejo Villavicencio barrels over these expectations and makes clear who she's writing for and why: 'hermanxs, it's time to fuck some shit up.' Refusing to turn people into 'subjects,' Villavicencio likens the act of translating her interviews with undocumented immigrants to translating a poem. This book is a revolution and revelation in narrative nonfiction that filled me with both rage and hope."

LAURA TAYLOR NAMEY

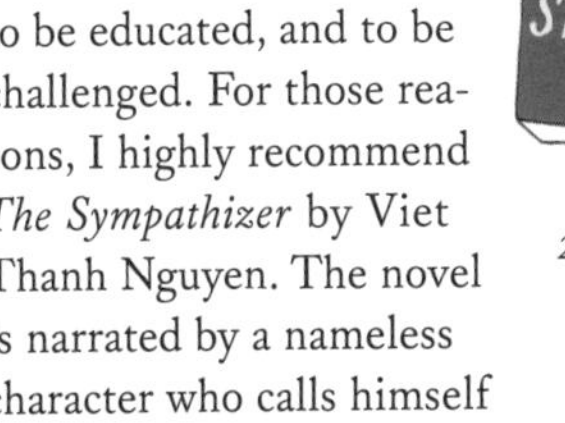

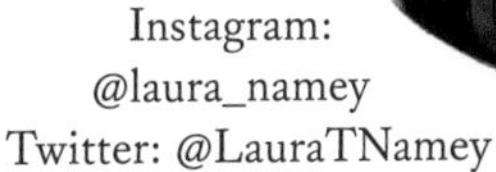

Author of *A Cuban Girl's Guide to Tea and Tomorrow*

Instagram:
@laura_namey
Twitter: @LauraTNamey

Little, Brown 2021 hardcover, art by Poppy Magda

Somewhere Between Bitter and Sweet
by Laekan Zea Kemp

"One step into the pages of *Somewhere Between Bitter and Sweet* will fill you with the pulse and grit of the diverse Austin food scene, and a tightly knit barrio struggling to survive and prosper. Here, the core of family is ripped open—its struggles, dreams, and misunderstandings. Experience the steam and sizzle of homemade Mexican food, and the sweetness of coconut cake and aspirations. Teens Penelope and Xander find love as they fight to reconcile their pasts, and work together to grow a bright future."

ESSAYS

Essays can cover any topic, and without a doubt you'll find something to pique your interest. Sometimes you read a book to learn and other times you read for entertainment. But there are times when you just need to read a book that makes you think. These books serve as pathways to inform, challenge societal norms, and survey humanity, and some will simply make you laugh.

When asked what she wants potential readers to know, Samantha Irby says that "despite how maybe gross and offensive my work may seem on the surface, that it really is accessible for lots of different types of people. But like, don't be scared by what people say about it. Give it a try." She writes the widely popular *Bitches Gotta Eat* blog and says that the best advice she would give to her younger self is "Just don't worry about it. I spent a lot of time worrying about things I couldn't change and that's just not helpful for anyone. Ride the wave. Getting stressed out about things that are beyond your control is the easiest trap."

Esmé Weijun Wang has an MFA in fiction and never planned to write nonfiction. Unaware that mental illness affected many members of her family, she was diagnosed with schizoaffective disorder in 2013 and late-stage Lyme disease in 2015. Wang reveals that she "inherited a love of writing and a talent for the visual arts from my mother, as well as her long and tapered fingers; I've also inherited a tendency for madness." When asked about writing *The Collected Schizophrenias* and the relationship between creativity and mental health, she emphasized that she "wants to be careful not to glamorize mental illness when it comes to creativity because more often than not it actually tends to inhibit creativity."

Graywolf Press 2019 paperback, design by Kimberly Glyder

Random House 2019 hardcover, design by Sharanya Durvasula

Jia Tolentino, a staff writer at the *New Yorker,* examines identity, the internet, and feminism in her debut collection, *Trick Mirror*. She describes the essays as "nine terrible children." When asked about the opening essay "The I in the Internet," Tolentino shared that she "tries to be on the Internet the way that I am in real life, which is unguarded and easy."

Valeria Luiselli based *Tell Me How It Ends: An Essay in Forty Questions* on her experience working as a translator for undocumented migrant children who risked their lives, mostly unaccompanied, to enter the United States from Central America and Mexico. Luiselli was responsible for asking the children 40 official U.S. immigration questions that would ultimately decide if they would be granted asylum or returned to the life they were trying to escape.

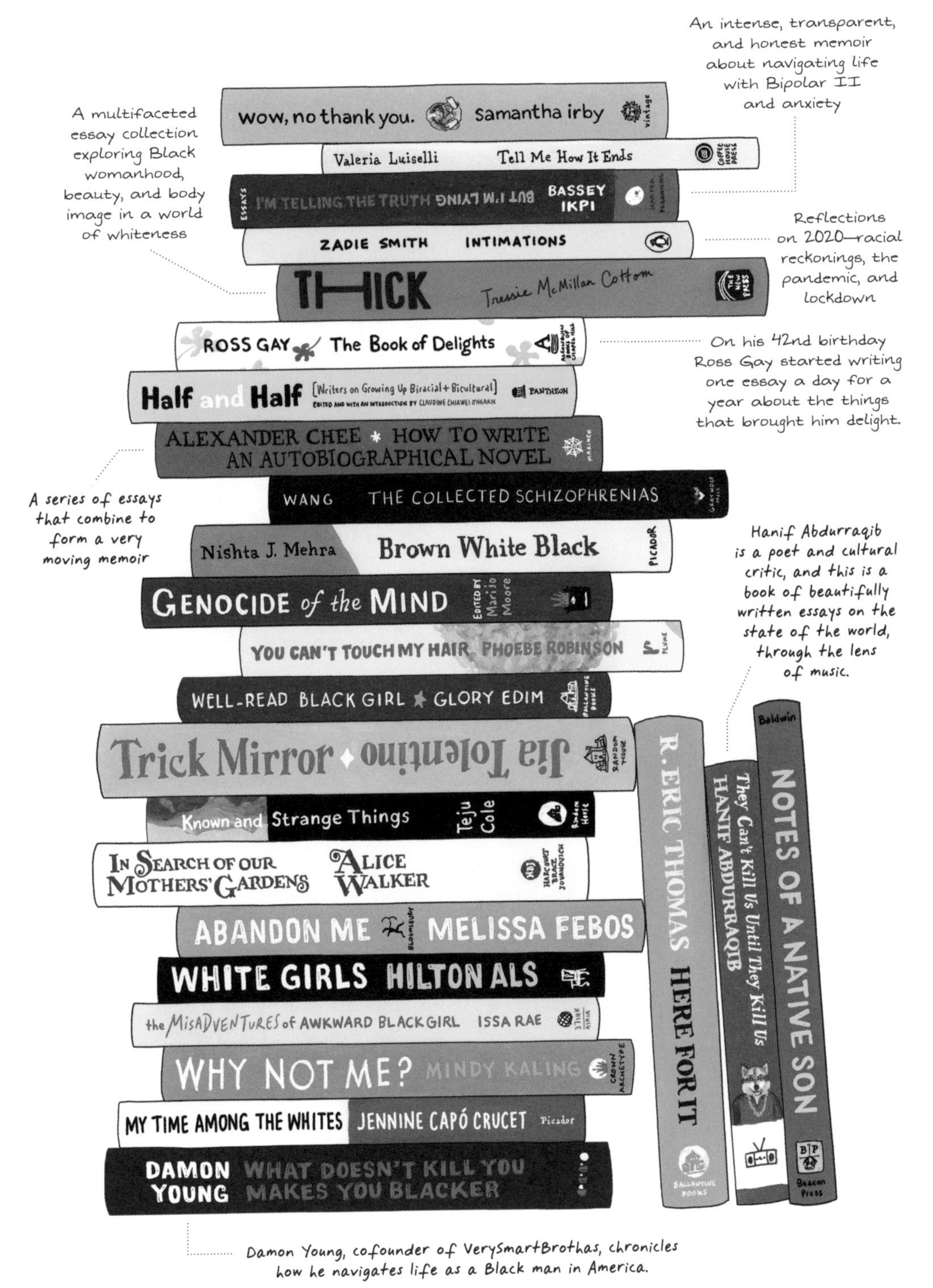
A multifaceted essay collection exploring Black womanhood, beauty, and body image in a world of whiteness
An intense, transparent, and honest memoir about navigating life with Bipolar II and anxiety
wow, no thank you. samantha irby vintage
Valeria Luiselli Tell Me How It Ends
ESSAYS I'M TELLING THE TRUTH BUT I'M LYING BASSEY IKPI
ZADIE SMITH INTIMATIONS
Reflections on 2020—racial reckonings, the pandemic, and lockdown
THICK Tressie McMillan Cottom THE NEW PRESS
ROSS GAY The Book of Delights
On his 42nd birthday Ross Gay started writing one essay a day for a year about the things that brought him delight.
Half and Half [Writers on Growing Up Biracial + Bicultural] EDITED AND WITH AN INTRODUCTION BY CLAUDINE CHIAWEI O'HEARN PANTHEON
ALEXANDER CHEE * HOW TO WRITE AN AUTOBIOGRAPHICAL NOVEL MARINER
A series of essays that combine to form a very moving memoir
WANG THE COLLECTED SCHIZOPHRENIAS
Nishta J. Mehra Brown White Black PICADOR
GENOCIDE of the MIND EDITED BY Marijo Moore
YOU CAN'T TOUCH MY HAIR PHOEBE ROBINSON PLUME
Hanif Abdurraqib is a poet and cultural critic, and this is a book of beautifully written essays on the state of the world, through the lens of music.
WELL-READ BLACK GIRL GLORY EDIM BALLANTINE BOOKS
Trick Mirror Jia Tolentino RANDOM HOUSE
Known and Strange Things Teju Cole Random House
IN SEARCH OF OUR MOTHERS' GARDENS ALICE WALKER HARCOURT BRACE JOVANOVICH
ABANDON ME BLOOMSBURY MELISSA FEBOS
WHITE GIRLS HILTON ALS
the MisADVENTURES of AWKWARD BLACK GIRL ISSA RAE
WHY NOT ME? MINDY KALING CROWN ARCHETYPE
MY TIME AMONG THE WHITES JENNINE CAPÓ CRUCET Picador
DAMON YOUNG WHAT DOESN'T KILL YOU MAKES YOU BLACKER
R. ERIC THOMAS HERE FOR IT BALLANTINE BOOKS
They Can't Kill Us Until They Kill Us HANIF ABDURRAQIB
Baldwin NOTES OF A NATIVE SON Beacon Press
Damon Young, cofounder of VerySmartBrothas, chronicles how he navigates life as a Black man in America.

BELOVED BOOKSTORES

A DIFFERENT BOOKLIST

Toronto, Ontario, Canada
Instagram: @adfrntbooklist

When you enter A Different Booklist, not only will you find shelves filled with books from the African Caribbean diaspora and the Global South, you will see walls lined with art and photography from local Black artists. This Canadian, independent, multicultural bookstore has been owned by husband-and-wife team Itah Sadu and Miguel San Vicente for more than two decades. Sadu, a renowned author and gifted storyteller, shares that "as an independent store, affirming yourself as a meeting place is so important."

SOLID STATE BOOKS

Washington, DC, USA
Instagram: @solidstatedc

Owners Scott Abel and Jake Cumsky-Whitlock opened this beloved neighborhood bookstore in 2017. Located in the bustling and historic H Street Corridor, they curate a diverse selection of fiction and nonfiction titles as well as an extensive children's and young adult selection. This vital social hub also features a coffee bar offering pastries, wine, and beer.

BIRCHBARK BOOKS

Minneapolis, Minnesota, USA
Instagram: @birchbark_books

Birchbark Books is owned by Louise Erdrich, award-winning author and enrolled member of the Turtle Mountain Band of Chippewa Indians. Located in the Twin Cities, Kenwood neighborhood, the store specializes in curating Native American titles for their shelves, and they also host events by Native and non-Native writers, journalists, and historians. Visitors entering the bookstore will see decor featuring genuine birch trees and a handcrafted canoe hanging from the ceiling. Along with the great Native literature, Birchbark deals directly with local, regional, and southwestern artisans to showcase Native art, handcrafted jewelry, basketry, quillwork, and paintings.

ESO WON BOOKS

Los Angeles, California, USA
Instagram: @esowonbooks

The southwest Los Angeles institution was opened in 1990 by James Fugate and Tom Hamilton. Growing up around books, Fugate realized the role Black people had played in the United States and around the world and wanted to be sure others knew that history too. Eso Won has become essential to its community; one customer described it as a barbershop where no one cuts hair. Fugate says sales have been up in 2020 and hopes people continue to support the store going forward. Ta-Nehisi Coates calls it his favorite bookstore and says, "It is part of the larger community of independent bookstores that writers celebrate, but its specific mission is to make sure [B]lack authors always have a home."

BOOKISH PEOPLE RECOMMEND

Dial 2021 paperback

POONAM MATHUR

Creator

Instagram:
@bookish.behavior

What We Carry
by Maya Shanbhag Lang

"The stories we tell ourselves keep us safe. Or so we believe. A story Maya Lang held tightly was one about the strength and brilliance of her mom. A woman who moved to a new country, built a successful career, and raised a family. What was not to admire? But the truth is never quite so dreamy. *What We Carry* is a beautifully written, deeply moving memoir about mothers and daughters, and the healing that occurs when you reckon with and work through the myths you've created about the person who raised you."

ANNA ISAAC

Bookstagrammer

Instagram:
@never_withouta_book

Corregidora
by Gayl Jones

Virago 2019 paperback, art by Lucinda Rogers

"Written as an internal monologue, as a stream of consciousness, *Corregidora* is not an easy read, but an important one. It underlines the most important aspect of slavery: the double marginalization of women on the plantations. James Baldwin said it best, '*Corregidora* is the most brutally honest and painful revelation of what has occurred, and is occurring, in the souls of Black men and women.' This novel is consequently structured around a complex sexual and literary antipathy between male-gendered violence and a female-gendered orality. Although it is short, this unique and revolutionary masterpiece considers difficult themes of generational trauma, preservation of memory, domestic and sexual violence, and womanhood and motherhood. An absolute must read."

Bloomsbury 2017 paperback, design by Patti Ratchford, photo by Tamara Staples

JESS LEE

Director, Learning Projects at City Year

Instagram:
@literaryintersections

White Rage: The Unspoken Truth of Our Racial Divide
by Carol Anderson

"Racism and white supremacy are written into our laws, 'working the halls of power' as Carol Anderson says in *White Rage*. Anderson connects our history of slavery, Reconstruction, and Jim Crow with the racism and white supremacy we are seeing play out daily. Read this book to begin to understand how lawmakers have used the law to keep hold of power, continue fostering white supremacy, and support their own 'white rage.' This book changed my life and I hope it helps to change yours as well."

MARISSA VINING

Attorney

Instagram:
@allegedlymari

I Am Not Your Perfect Mexican Daughter
by Erika L. Sánchez

Ember 2019 paperback, art by Connie Gabbert

"This book introduces you to Julia, a teenager struggling to understand why her parents don't want more for their lives. It wasn't until my reread of this book that I deeply connected with Julia as a daughter of immigrants born in the United States. We see Julia chasing the American Dream while trying to still follow strict Mexican traditions and customs. That in-between-ness I have felt my entire life was so clearly portrayed in each page. This book gets overlooked for being YA, but it is deep and tackles a lot of important topics."

Katherine Tegen 2018 hardcover, design by Erin Fitzsimmons

AJ SANDERS

Literary influencer

Instagram:
@readingwithglamour

Monday's Not Coming
by Tiffany D. Jackson

"There are a few books that live rent-free in mind and this YA novel is one. It follows Claudia Coleman as she searches for her best friend Monday. This is an intense read with a splash of horror that will definitely keep you on your toes. During the entire book I kept asking myself, 'Where is Monday?' Evoking an array of emotions from the reader, Jackson does an amazing job of keeping the plot interesting and suspenseful while also shining the light on the lack of national media coverage when Black girls go missing. I've read many books, and this one is at the top of my highly recommended list."

DEIRDRE (DIDI) BORIE

Creator of #readsoullit and The Read Soul Lit Book Club

Instagram:
@browngirlreading,
@readsoullit
Twitter: @ReadEngDee
YouTube:
Brown Girl Reading

Thomas Dunne 2009 hardcover, art by Dudley Vaccianna

Daughters of the Stone
by Dahlma Llanos-Figueroa

"The ultimate Black Girl Magic book, *Daughters of the Stone* is the story of five generations of women and how they manage their gifts. This novel of connections between mothers and daughters takes us on a journey of love, culture, history, and power. Fela, victim of the Atlantic slave trade, transported from Nigeria to Puerto Rico, is the beginning of the generations of Afro-Puerto Rican women who will struggle to understand and use their gifts. The author teaches us about race, spirituality, and survival because when all seems lost, the only thing left is the stone."

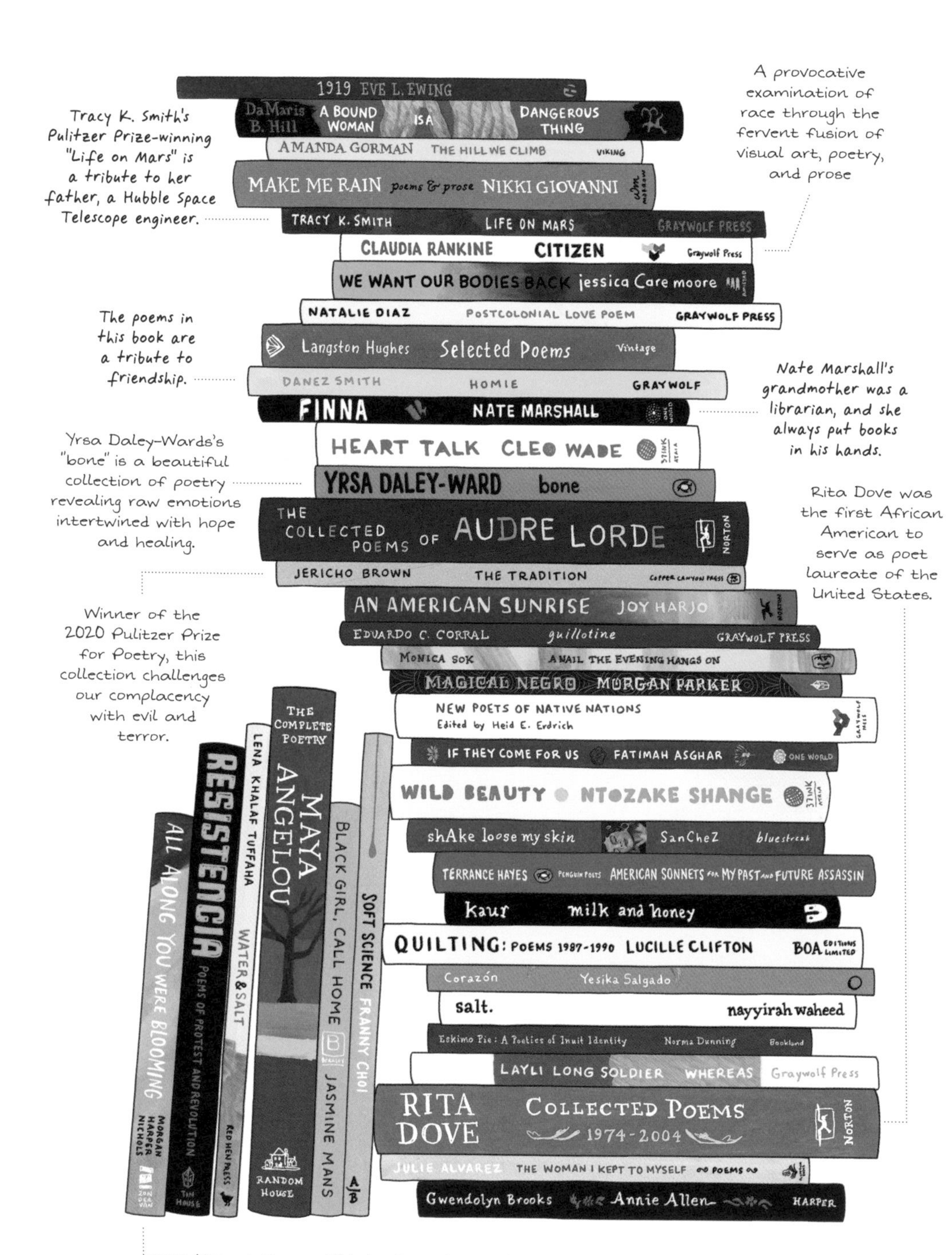

1919 EVE L. EWING
DaMaris B. Hill A BOUND WOMAN IS A DANGEROUS THING
AMANDA GORMAN THE HILL WE CLIMB VIKING
MAKE ME RAIN poems & prose NIKKI GIOVANNI
TRACY K. SMITH LIFE ON MARS GRAYWOLF PRESS
CLAUDIA RANKINE CITIZEN Graywolf Press
WE WANT OUR BODIES BACK jessica Care moore
NATALIE DIAZ POSTCOLONIAL LOVE POEM GRAYWOLF PRESS
Langston Hughes Selected Poems Vintage
DANEZ SMITH HOMIE GRAYWOLF
FINNA NATE MARSHALL
HEART TALK CLEO WADE
YRSA DALEY-WARD bone
THE COLLECTED POEMS OF AUDRE LORDE NORTON
JERICHO BROWN THE TRADITION COPPER CANYON PRESS
AN AMERICAN SUNRISE JOY HARJO NORTON
EDUARDO C. CORRAL guillotine GRAYWOLF PRESS
MONICA SOK A NAIL THE EVENING HANGS ON
MAGICAL NEGRO MORGAN PARKER
NEW POETS OF NATIVE NATIONS Edited by Heid E. Erdrich
IF THEY COME FOR US FATIMAH ASGHAR ONE WORLD
WILD BEAUTY NTOZAKE SHANGE
shAke loose my skin SanCheZ bluestreak
TERRANCE HAYES PENGUIN POETS AMERICAN SONNETS FOR MY PAST AND FUTURE ASSASSIN
kaur milk and honey
QUILTING: POEMS 1987-1990 LUCILLE CLIFTON BOA EDITIONS LIMITED
Corazón Yesika Salgado
salt. nayyirah waheed
Eskimo Pie: A Poetics of Inuit Identity Norma Dunning Bookland
LAYLI LONG SOLDIER WHEREAS Graywolf Press
RITA DOVE COLLECTED POEMS 1974-2004 NORTON
JULIE ALVAREZ THE WOMAN I KEPT TO MYSELF POEMS
Gwendolyn Brooks Annie Allen HARPER
ALL ALONG YOU WERE BLOOMING MORGAN HARPER NICHOLS ZONDERVAN
RESISTENCIA POEMS OF PROTEST AND REVOLUTION TIN HOUSE
LENA KHALAF TUFFAHA WATER & SALT RED HEN PRESS
THE COMPLETE POETRY MAYA ANGELOU RANDOM HOUSE
BLACK GIRL, CALL HOME JASMINE MANS BERKLEY
SOFT SCIENCE FRANNY CHOI A/B
Tracy K. Smith's Pulitzer Prize-winning "Life on Mars" is a tribute to her father, a Hubble Space Telescope engineer.
A provocative examination of race through the fervent fusion of visual art, poetry, and prose
The poems in this book are a tribute to friendship.
Nate Marshall's grandmother was a librarian, and she always put books in his hands.
Yrsa Daley-Wards's "bone" is a beautiful collection of poetry revealing raw emotions intertwined with hope and healing.
Rita Dove was the first African American to serve as poet laureate of the United States.
Winner of the 2020 Pulitzer Prize for Poetry, this collection challenges our complacency with evil and terror.
Morgan Harper Nichols started pursuing her passion for writing, art, and design while touring as a full-time musician and singer-songwriter.

POETRY

Poetry has the power to make you feel seen and can also pierce your heart. The cultural rhythm, harmony of language, and lyrical prose emerging from poems illuminate stories that may otherwise go unseen and elevate marginalized voices.

Harper 1949 hardcover

Gwendolyn Brooks won the Pulitzer Prize for Poetry for *Annie Allen* in 1950, making her the first African American to be awarded the prize. Brooks published her first poem in a children's magazine at the age of 13 and published 75 poems by the time she turned 16. She became a regular contributor to the *Chicago Defender,* an iconic Black newspaper, at the age of 17.

In 2014, Amanda Gorman was named the first Los Angeles Youth Poet Laureate and in 2017, became the first-ever National Youth Poet Laureate. Gorman captured the hearts of people in the United States and around the world when she eloquently delivered an electrifying reading of her poem, *The Hill We Climb*, at President Joe Biden's inauguration. As the youngest presidential inaugural poet in United States history, her inspiring words permeated the social fabric of society. In 2021, she became the first poet to ever perform during a Super Bowl (Super Bowl LV).

Viking Books 2021 hardcover, design by Jim Hoover

Yesika Salgado describes herself as a "Salvadoran poet who writes about her family, her culture, her city, and her fat brown body." Her poetry collection *Corazón* is a love story, and she believes that "many of us experience heartbreak more than once, so the fact that you keep going back to love, despite heartbreak, is a beautiful miracle. Instead of feeling ashamed of it, I want to acknowledge the beauty there is to love after love keeps hurting you."

Not a Cult 2018 paperback, design by Cassidy Trier

It's been said that Rupi Kaur used social media to transform how readers consume poetry. Inspired by her mother to paint and draw, Kaur rose to fame by sharing her short visual poetry on Tumblr and Instagram. Her debut collection, *Milk and Honey,* has sold over five million copies worldwide and has been translated into more than 35 languages. During the Covid-19 pandemic she released her third poetry collection, *Home Body.*

Andrews McMeel 2015 paperback

In 2019, the Library of Congress appointed Joy Harjo as the United States Poet Laureate, the first Native American to hold that honor. Harjo is a member of the Muscogee (Creek) Nation. *An American Sunrise* explores family, the history of her people, and their removal from their land (what is now Oklahoma).

In addition to being a poet, Harjo is a singer and plays the saxophone and flute with Arrow Dynamics Band. →

BOOKS IN VERSE

These works use poetry (sometimes mixed with prose and illustration) to tell a narrative and often explore life-changing events and difficult topics with sensitivity. They include novels, memoirs, and biographies, and while many are written for young adult and middle-grade readers, they are enjoyed by people of all ages.

Puffin 2016 paperback, design by Theresa Evangelista

BROWN GIRL DREAMING

by Jacqueline Woodson

A compelling memoir of Woodson's childhood as an African American girl in 1960s South Carolina and New York.

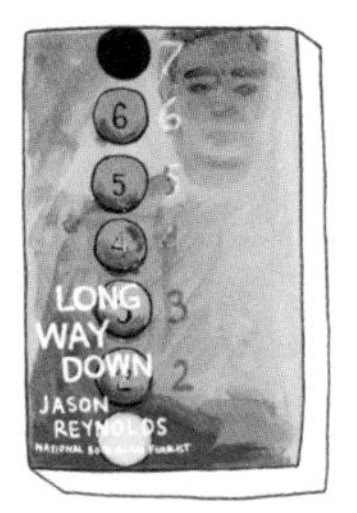

Atheneum 2017 hardcover, design by Michael McCartney

LONG WAY DOWN

by Jason Reynolds

A 15-year-old named Will seeks to avenge his 19-year-old brother's death.

INSIDE OUT & BACK AGAIN

by Thanhhà Lại

HarperCollins 2013 paperback, design by Ray Shappell, art by Zdenko Bašić & Manuel Šumberac

A novel influenced by the author's fleeing Vietnam after the Fall of Saigon and immigrating to Alabama as a child.

Quill Tree Books 2020 hardcover, design by Erin Fitzsimmons, art by Bijou Karman

CLAP WHEN YOU LAND

by Elizabeth Acevedo

Camino and Yahaira discover they are sisters when their beloved father dies in a plane crash.

HarperCollins 2021 hardcover, design by Corina Lupp, art by Ceres Lau

IF I TELL YOU THE TRUTH

by Jasmin Kaur

The story of Kiran, a Punjabi Sikh teenager who becomes pregnant after being sexually assaulted.

Balzer & Bray 2020 hardcover, design by Jenna Stempel-Lobell, art by Adriana Bellet

THE BLACK FLAMINGO

by Dean Atta

A coming-of-age story about Michael, a mixed-race gay teen in London.

MUTED

by Tami Charles

Inspired by real-life events, this novel explores the sinister nature of the music industry.

Scholastic Press 2021 hardcover, design by Maeve Norton, art by Adekunle Gold

OTHER WORDS FOR HOME

by Jasmine Warga

Jude, a 12-year-old Syrian refugee, moves to America with her mother, leaving behind her father and brother.

Balzer & Bray 2019 hardcover, design by Jenna Stempel-Lobell, art by Anoosha Syed

REBOUND

by Kwame Alexander

The story of Charlie Bell, the father in Alexander's Newbery-winning novel *The Crossover*.

Houghton Mifflin Harcourt 2018 hardcover, design by Lisa Vega & Sammy Yuen

WITH A STAR IN MY HAND

by Margarita Engle

A biography of Nicaraguan poet Rubén Darío.

Atheneum 2020 hardcover, design by Debra Sfetsios-Conover, art by Willian Santiago

Dutton 2020 hardcover, art by Rachelle Baker

EVERY BODY LOOKING

by Candice Iloh

A Nigerian American teen navigates the freedom of self-discovery and the expectations of her family during her first year of college.

Crown 2021 hardcover, design by Ray Shappell & Torborg Davern, art by Kgabo Mametja

CHLORINE SKY

by Mahogany L. Browne

A debut novel about friendship, based on Browne's experiences in high school.

HEALING

How do we heal our minds and bodies from the trauma caused by living in a troubled and often unjust society? How do we heal our relationship with the natural world? How do we heal our creative souls and learn to express ourselves freely? These books are here for you.

Chronicle Books 2020 hardcover, design by Vanessa Dina

Alexandra Elle's *After the Rain* is a guidebook: a set of 15 lessons (with titles like Change, Self-Love, Validation, and Family) that are also short memoirs, completed with poetic meditations and healing practices. Elle discovered writing as a preteen, encouraged by a therapist to soothe and mend herself with words, and she later sparked an Instagram phenomenon, posting pictures of her affirmations and gentle reminders on Post-it "notes to self." To Elle, the definition of self-care is "filling yourself up so you can pour into others," and the goal of her book is to "help support people in finding their voices and standing close to their truths without guilt or shame."

Arianna Davis has had a passion for writing since early in life. Always a big reader, she grew up on books like *The Baby-Sitters Club*. Now the senior director of editorial and strategy at *Oprah Daily*, Davis shared that "being Latinx and growing up with a Puerto Rican mother, I was aware of [Mexican artist] Frida [Kahlo], but it wasn't until I was in high school that the lifelong fascination began." Davis hopes that her debut book, *What Would Frida Do?*, "inspires readers to be bolder and live life a little more."

In *My Grandmother's Hands*, Resmaa Menakem explains how trauma affects our bodies as much or more than our minds, and how we must deal with that to move forward. The title refers to when, as a boy, he noticed his grandmother's hands were very thick, from picking cotton as a sharecropper's daughter beginning at age four. Menakem studied with a psychiatrist, a psychologist, and a neuroscientist before writing the book, and used his knowledge to create simple methods people can use to address such trauma, building on ancient practices and developing new ones. These methods are for everyone, and Menakem feels that "'the racial divide' is not an obstacle to be conquered; it's a wound that lives inside our bodies—a wound we can heal."

Central Recovery Press 2017 paperback, design by The Book Designers

Aimee Nezhukumatathil, born in Chicago to a Filipina mother and Malayali Indian father, has authored four poetry collections. *World of Wonders* is her first book of prose: illustrated essays on nature and how its creatures can inspire us in our everyday lives. For instance, how the axolotl, a boneless underwater salamander, can show us how to smile through everything, even when "a white girl tries to tell you what your brown skin can and cannot wear for makeup."

LALAH DELIA VIBRATE HIGHER DAILY
How to make uplifting choices, every day
Williams | Owens | Syedullah RADICAL DHARMA
IWÍGARA ENRIQUE SALMÓN
CLEO WADE WHERE TO BEGIN
A collection of uplifting ideas, mantras, and poems for when you are feeling overwhelmed by worry, fear, anxiety, or helplessness
Small Doses Amanda Seales
A guide to decluttering your life and making space for what really matters
THE AFROMINIMALIST'S GUIDE TO LIVING WITH LESS CHRISTINE PLATT
KIMMERER BRAIDING SWEETGRASS
How to Do Nothing Jenny Odell
As a licensed therapist, Nedra Glover Tawwab provides tools to help set boundaries in your relationships.
SET BOUNDARIES, FIND PEACE a guide to reclaiming yourself NEDRA GLOVER TAWWAB
THE RACIAL HEALING HANDBOOK SINGH
Amalia Andrade's workbook for dealing with fear and anxiety is funny, charming, and big-hearted.
AMALIA ANDRADE THINGS YOU THINK ABOUT WHEN YOU BITE YOUR NAILS
My Grandmother's Hands MENAKEM
YOUR ILLUSTRATED GUIDE TO BECOMING ONE WITH THE UNIVERSE SAKUGAWA
Dreamy illustrations and metaphysical lessons for connecting
NEZHUKUMATATHIL WORLD OF WONDERS milkweed editions
In her memoir, Shonda Rhimes steps out of her comfort zone and says yes to the things that scare her.
THE BODY IS NOT AN APOLOGY SONYA RENEE TAYLOR
Dwellings LINDA HOGAN
MINDFUL OF RACE RUTH KING
Badass Black Girl Quotes, Questions, and Affirmations for Teens M.J.Fievre
The PATH Made CLEAR Discovering Your Life's Direction and Purpose OPRAH WINFREY
EARTH KEEPER N. Scott Momaday
NATIVE KAITLIN B. CURTICE
own your glow LATHAM THOMAS
JUSTINA BLAKENEY THE NEW BOHEMIANS HANDBOOK ABRAMS
adrienne maree brown PLEASURE ACTIVISM The Politics of Feeling Good
JESSAMYN STANLEY EVERY BODY YOGA workman
PEACE IS EVERY STEP Thich Nhat Hanh
YEAR OF YES SHONDA RHIMES
From Scratch Tembi Locke
FINNEY BLACK FACES, WHITE SPACES Reimagining the Relationship of African Americans to the Great Outdoors
ARIANNA DAVIS WHAT WOULD FRIDA DO?
START WHERE YOU ARE meera lee patel
ELLE AFTER the RAIN CHRONICLE BOOKS
A memoir about falling in love, and into and out of grief, set in Sicily
Carolyn Finney examines the relationship both Black and white people have with the great outdoors and how and why it differs.

BELOVED BOOKSTORES

THE LIT. BAR

Bronx, New York, USA
Instagram: @thelitbar

When Noëlle Santos, a former human resources director, learned that the only bookstore in the Bronx was closing, she took action. Her petition to save the bookstore failed, but that did not deter her. Born and raised in the Bronx, Santos set her wheels in motion to make her dream of opening a bookstore and wine bar come to fruition. With the tagline "bookstore and chill," Santos's dreams came true on April 27, 2019, Independent Bookstore Day, when the Lit. Bar opened. The venue encourages curious readers and welcomes literary and community gatherings—while the wine bar connects the great pastimes of social sipping and introverted reading. Upon entering the space, guests take in the stunning views featuring a crystal chandelier and a mural of a Black girl reading. The Lit. Bar is the *only* indie bookstore in the borough, which is home to 1.5 million residents.

ACKNOWLEDGMENTS

Making a book in 2020—a book full of inspiring stories—gave us a spark of clear purpose in a murky, dismal time. Collaborating across many time zones cured the isolation caused by the pandemic and provided us with much joy. This book would not exist without many wonderful people putting time and love into it, and we are incredibly grateful to all of them. We give huge thanks to our agent, Kate Woodrow, and enormous thanks to our two brilliant editors Dena Rayess and Sahara Clement; you all were a joy to meet with every week (even when we were slightly behind on crazy deadlines!). And, of course, we give colossal thanks to designer Kristen Hewitt and production developer Erin Thacker, for putting it all together in the most beautiful way. We are grateful to Christina Amini for sharing our vision and making it happen, and to copyeditor Shasta Clinch and proofreaders Marie Oishi and Ariela Rudy Zaltzman for helping us make it right.

Jamise: I don't believe I would have taken the leap to write a book and because of Jane Mount here I am! I owe a debt of gratitude to Jane for inviting me to take this journey with her. This has been one of the greatest, most stressful yet joyful times in my life. In the midst of writing during a pandemic, one highlight was our weekly video meetings that gave me the push I needed to get through the day or when I felt overwhelmed with research. I'm immensely grateful to Tayari Jones and Linda Claude-Oben, Esq., for their guidance and advice. None of this would be possible without my life anchors: Alexis Harper, Alvin Harper Jr., Dorothy Vaughn, JaMiko Sapp, Mercedes Sapp, and Warren Sapp II, thank you for providing me with endless love, support and laughter; to James Bryson for consistently pouring into me the love that keeps me elevated and for feeding me when I forgot to eat while writing. Lastly, I dedicate this book to the loving memory of my father, Ret. SGM James R. Vaughn Jr., who always reminded me that you only get one go around in life, Make It Count!

Jane: I am profoundly grateful to Jamise for going on this book adventure with me (especially since we barely knew each other beforehand!). She jumped into it completely—despite the crazy amount of work and insane deadlines proposed—and made every stage of the process immensely better and more fun, even when we were both completely exhausted. I'm also extremely grateful to my mom, Sharon Mount, for helping with research and for her always encouraging words and welcome distractions. Many thanks and much love to Li Frei and Chaz Edlao, and to Madison, Charmaine, Kepler, and Phoenix Ehrhart-Mount for always being there. And thanks to Lada, Benz, and Opel for allowing me to bury my tired face in their fur when necessary. And most especially, thank you to Darko Karas for being my one, for always reminding me to just keep going, and for making everything worth it.

BIBLIOGRAPHY & CREDITS

(IN ORDER OF APPEARANCE)

Clemens, Sara. "Celebrate the 60th Anniversary of *Things Fall Apart*." *Penguin Random House Higher Education*, Penguin Random House, August 22, 2018. penguinrandomhousehighereducation.com/2018/08/22/things-fall-apart-60th-anniversary.

Griffin, Farah Jasmine. "Brief Life of Novelist Ann Petry." *Harvard Magazine*, Harvard University, December 16, 2013. www.harvardmagazine.com/2014/01/ann-petry.

Edwards, Brent Hayes. "A Legless Black Man Comes into a Windfall in This Biting Satire." Review of *Romance in Marseilles*, by Claude McKay. *New York Times*, February 11, 2020, Book Review section. www.nytimes.com/2020/02/11/books/review/romance-in-marseilles-claude-mckay.html.

Cisneros, Sandra. "*The House on Mango Street*—The Story." Uploaded by knopfgroup, April 1, 2009. YouTube video, 3:50. www.youtube.com/watch?v=0Pyf89VsNmg.

Hosseini, Khaled. "*Kite Runner* Author on His Childhood, His Writing, and the Plight of Afghan Refugees." Interview with *RadioFreeEurope/RadioLiberty*, June 21, 2012. www.rferl.org/a/interview-kite-runner-afghan-emigre-writer-khaled-hosseini/24621078.html.

Ishiguro, Kazuo. "Kazuo Ishiguro: *Never Let Me Go*." Interview with Karen Grigsby Bates, National Public Radio, May 4, 2005. www.npr.org/transcripts/4629918.

Cordero, Rosy. "*Bodega Dreams* author on overcoming 'systemic racism' in publishing 20 years ago, and today." *Entertainment Weekly*, March 23, 2020. https://ew.com/books bodega-dreams-anniversary-ernesto-quinonez.

Alvarez, Julia. "Meet Julia." Author website, accessed January 17, 2021. www.juliaalvarez.com/about.

"*Their Eyes Were Watching God*." Wikipedia, the Free Encyclopedia, Wikimedia Foundation, Inc. Last modified February 3, 2021. en.wikipedia.org/wiki/Their_Eyes_Were_Watching_God.

Walker, Alice. Cover endorsement for *Their Eyes Were Watching God*, by Zora Neale Hurston. New York: HarperCollins, 2013.

Smith, Zadie. Cover endorsement for *Their Eyes Were Watching God*, by Zora Neale Hurston. London: Virago Modern Classics, 2018.

Winfrey, Oprah. Introduction [TBC]. *Their Eyes Were Watching God*. DVD. Directed by Darnell Martin. Chicago: Harpo Productions, 2005.

Dougher, Patrick. "About the Artist." Artist website. Accessed February 17, 2021. www.godbodyart.com/about-the-artist.

Ibelle, Jackson Ferrari. "Cafe Con Libros Boxes Out Amazon in Support of Indie Bookstores." *BK Reader*, October 21, 2020. www.bkreader.com/2020/10/21/brooklyns-cafe-con-libros-boxes-out-amazon-in-support-of-indie-bookstores.

Wheeler, André. "'Economic Duress Is Nothing New': Can America's Oldest Black Bookstore Survive the Pandemic?" *The Guardian*, May 15, 2020. www.theguardian.com/books/2020/may/15/marcus-books-oakland-oldest-black-bookstore.

Washington, Bryan. "The Year in Broth." *Hazlitt*, December 10, 2018. hazlitt.net/feature/year-broth.

Gowdy, ShaCamree. "Houston Author Bryan Washington Lands TV Deal for Debut Novel *Memorial*." *Chron.com*, the website of the *Houston Chronicle*, October 19, 2020. www.chron.com/entertainment/article/Houston-author-Bryan-Washington-lands-TV-deal-for-15658590.php.

Persaud, Ingrid. "That Is Where My Navel String Buried: An Interview with Ingrid Persaud." Interview with Will Forrester. *PEN Transmissions*, May 12, 2020. pentransmissions.com/2020/05/12/that-is-where-my-navel-string-buried-an-interview-with-ingrid-persaud.

Kim, Angie. "Angie Kim: On Being a Full-Time Writer, HBOT Therapy and her debut novel, *Miracle Creek*." Interview with Kailey Brennan. Write or Die Tribe, September 3, 2019. www.writeordietribe.com/author-interviews/interview-with-angie-kim.

Choo, Yangsze."Interview with an Author: Yangsze Choo" Interview with Daryl M., Los Angeles Public Library (blog), May 9, 2019. www.lapl.org/collections-resources/blogs/lapl/interview-author-yangsze-choo.

McBride, James. "James McBride: *Deacon King Kong* showcases the brilliance that happens when a great writer feels creatively free." Interview with Langston Collin Wilkins. *BookPage*, March 2020. bookpage.com/interviews/24847-james-mcbride-fiction#.X7qN78hKg2w.

Askaripour, Mateo. "Mateo Askaripour on His Darkly Comic Debut Novel." Interview with Scott Simon, *Weekend Edition*, National Public Radio, January 2, 2021. www.npr.org/2021/01/02/952807025/mateo-askaripour-on-his-darkly-comic-debut-novel.

Perez, Lexy. "*The Vanishing Half* Author Brit Bennett Unpacks Novel's Take on Race: 'Identity Is Complicated.'" *Hollywood Reporter*, August 11, 2020. www.hollywoodreporter.com/news/vanishing-author-brit-bennett-unpacks-novels-take-race-identity-is-complicated-1305774.

Kim, Nancy Jooyoun. "Author Interview: Nancy Jooyoun Kim." Interview with Kelsey Norris. Libro.fm Audiobooks, August 25, 2020. blog.libro.fm/author-interview-nancy-jooyoun-kim.

Fassler, Joe. "What Writers Can Take Away from the Bible." *The Atlantic*, December 20, 2017. www.theatlantic.com/entertainment/archive/2017/12/min-jin-lee-by-heart/548810.

Oyeyemi, Helen. "Bookforum Talks with Helen Oyeyemi." Interview with Heather Akumiah. *Bookforum*, June 20, 2016.

Quinn, Annalisa. "The Professionally Haunted Life of Helen Oyeyemi." Book News and Features, National Public Radio, March 7, 2014. www.npr.org/2014/03/07/282065410/the-professionally-haunted-life-of-helen-oyeyemi.

Oyeyemi, Helen. "Helen Oyeyemi: 'I'm Interested in the Way Women Disappoint One Another.'" Interview with Liz Hoggard. *The Guardian*, March 2, 2014. www.theguardian.com/books/2014/mar/02/helen-oyeyemi-women-disappoint-one-another.

Mbue, Imbolo. "The Hawaii of *Sharks in the Time of Saviors* Is Modern, Yet Mystical." *New York Times*, March 30, 2020. www.nytimes.com/2020/03/30/books/review/kawai-strong-washburn-sharks-in-the-time-of-saviors.html.

Washburn, Kawai Strong. "Be Bludgeoned with the Wonder: An Interview with Kawai Strong Washburn on *Sharks in the Time of Saviors*." Interview with J. David Gonzalez. *Los Angeles Review of Books*, March 6, 2020. lareviewofbooks.org/article/be-bludgeoned-with-the-wonder-an-interview-with-kawai-strong-washburn-on-sharks-in-the-time-of-saviors.

Aldrich, Margret. "Why Sharing Diverse Books in Little Free Libraries Matters." Little Free Library website. Accessed July 15, 2020. littlefreelibrary.org/why-sharing-diverse-books-in-little-free-libraries-matters.

MPR News Staff. "*The Book of Harlan*: Following a Black Musician Caught up in WWII." MPR News, June 7, 2016. www.mprnews.org/story/2016/06/07/books-book-of-harlan.

Lefferts, Daniel. "With Her New Book, Kaitlyn Greenidge Practices Radical Care." *Publishers Weekly*, November 20, 2020. www.publishersweekly.com/pw/by-topic/authors/profiles/article/84948-with-her-new-book-kaitlyn-greenidge-practices-radical-care.html.

"Susan Abulhawa." Ayesha Pande Literary. Accessed January 18, 2021. www.pandeliterary.com/susan-abulhawa.

"Discover the 5 Under 35 Honorees 2016." National Book Foundation. Accessed January 18, 2021. www.nationalbook.org/awards-prizes/5-under-35-2016.

"Margaret Walker." *Encyclopaedia Britannica Online*. Accessed November 26, 2020. www.britannica.com/biography/Margaret-Walker.

Kenan, Randall. "A Conversation with Randall Kenan." Interview with Sheryl Cornett. *Image* 48. imagejournal.org/article/a-conversation-with-randall-kenan.

Kahakauwila, Kristiana. "A Conversation with Kristiana Kahakauwila about *This is Paradise*." Interview with Bill Wolfe. Read Her Like an Open Book, March 22, 2014. readherlikeanopenbook.com/2014/03/22/a-conversation-with-kristiana-kahakauwila-about-this-is-paradise.

Thompson-Spires, Nafissa. "Nafissa Thompson-Spires: 'I Wanted to See More Stories about Nerdy Black People.'" Interview with Anita Sethi. *The Guardian*, August 3, 2019. www.theguardian.com/books/2019/aug/03/nafissa-thompson-spires-interview-heads-of-the-colored-people.

Doyon, Marie. "A Conversation with N. K. Jemisin on New York, the Homogenization of Whiteness, and The City We Became." *Chronogram*, April 30, 2020. www.chronogram.com/hudsonvalley/a-conversation-with-n-k-jemisin-on-new-york-the-homogenization-of-whiteness-and-the-city-we-became/Content?oid=10508607.

Matthews, Cate. "Author N. K. Jemisin on Race, Gentrification and the Power of Fiction to Bring People Together." *Time*, March 13, 2020. time.com/5802555/nk-jemisin-the-city-we-became.

"Why Cherie Dimaline Calls on Her Indigenous Heritage as a Bestselling Storyteller and Writer." CBC, CBC Books, June 23, 2020. www.cbc.ca/books/why-cherie-dimaline-calls-on-her-indigenous-heritage-as-a-bestselling-storyteller-and-writer-1.5604533.

Monday, Caitlin. "Q&A with Darcie Little Badger, *Elatsoe*." We Need Diverse Books, November 2, 2020. diversebooks.org/qa-with-darcie-little-badger-elatsoe.

Kim, Na. "Illustrator and Art Director Na Kim on Good Design, Avoiding Trends, and Staying Creatively Engaged." The Creative Independent. Accessed February 17, 2021. thecreativeindependent.com/people/illustrator-and-art-director-na-kim-on-good-design-avoiding-trends-and-staying-creatively-engaged.

Petit, Zachary. "When Your Book Design Career Starts at Age 10 and Peaks at *Crazy, Rich Asians*." *Eye on Design*, February 28, 2019. eyeondesign.aiga.org/when-your-book-design-career-starts-at-age-10-and-peeks-at-crazy-rich-asians.

"Behind the Book Covers with Riverhead's Grace." Penguin Random House website, July 27, 2017. global.penguinrandomhouse.com/announcements/behind-the-book-covers-with-riverheads-grace-han.

Huang, Linda."Don't Judge a Book by Its Cover with Linda Huang." Interview with Adam T. Blackbourn (blog), January 31, 2016. www.adamblackbourn.com/song/2016/1/13/g-dont-judge-a-book-by-its-cover-with-linda-huang.

"Semicolon Is Chicago's Newest Bookstore." Chicago Review of Books, August 25, 2019. chireviewofbooks.com/2019/08/25/semicolon-is-chicagos-newest-bookstore.

Trimble, Lynn. "Supporters Are Working to Save Palabras Bilingual Bookstore in." *Phoenix New Times*, May 25, 2020. www.phoenixnewtimes.com/arts/why-supporters-are-working-to-save-palabras-bilingual-bookstore-in-phoenix-11471990.

Ramji, Shazia Hafiz. "Vancouver's Massy Books Is Both Welcomed and Welcoming." *Quill and Quire*, April 26, 2018. quillandquire.com/omni/vancouvers-massy-books-is-both-welcomed-and-welcoming.

Donnella, Leah. "YA Fantasy Where The Oppression Is Real." *Code Switch*, National Public Radio, January 28, 2020. www.npr.org/sections/codeswitch/2020/01/28/800167671/ya-fantasy-where-the-oppression-is-real.

Duspiva, Alyssa. "R.F. Kuang Stuns with Her Debut Fantasy Novel, *The Poppy War*." *RT Book Reviews*, March 26, 2018. web.archive.org/web/20180513011422/https://www.rtbookreviews.com/bonus-content/q-a/the-poppy-war-rf-kuang.

Oldfield, Kate. "Jordan Ifueko on Her Stunning Debut West African Inspired YA Fantasy, *Raybearer*." United By Pop, August 30, 2020. www.unitedbypop.com/young-adult-books/interviews-young-adult-books/jordan-ifueko-raybearer.

Oshiro, Mark. "Interview with Mark Oshiro." Interview with Jackie Balbastro. Pine Reads Review, September 25, 2020. www.pinereadsreview.com/blog/interview-with-mark-oshiro.

Lea, Richard. "Oyinkan Braithwaite's serial-killer thriller: would you help your murderer sister?" *The Guardian*, January 15, 2019. www.theguardian.com/books/2019/jan/15/oyinkan-braithwaite-thriller-nigerian-author-comic-debut-novel-my-sister-the-serial-killer.

Braithwaite, Oyinkan. "Stuck with Them: An Interview with Oyinkan Braithwaite." Interview with Ayọ̀bámi Adébáyọ̀. *Los Angeles Review of Books*, January 11, 2019. lareviewofbooks.org/article/stuck-with-them-an-interview-with-oyinkan-braithwaite.

Moreno-Garcia, Silvia. "The PEN Ten: An Interview with Silvia Moreno-Garcia." Interview with Jared Jackson, PEN America, July 9, 2020. pen.org/the-pen-ten-silvia-moreno-garcia/.

LaValle, Victor. "The Craft Is All the Same: A Conversation with Victor LaValle." Interview with Ayize Jama-Everett. *Los Angeles Review of Books*, November 22, 2018. lareviewofbooks.org/article/the-craft-is-all-the-same-a-conversation-with-victor-lavalle.

Matheson, Nadine. "An Interview with Nadine Matheson." Interview with Harrogate International Festivals. Accessed April 28, 2021. harrogateinternationalfestivals.com/youre-booked-online/an-interview-with-nadine-matheson/.

"Lin-Manuel Miranda's Sonnet from the Tony Awards." *New York Times*, June 13, 2016. www.nytimes.com/2016/06/13/theater/lin-manuel-mirandas-sonnet-from-the-tony-awards.html.

Chung, Nicole. "*The Kiss Quotient* Is a Perfect Romantic Equation." *Shondaland*, June 5, 2018. www.shondaland.com/inspire/books/a21052691/the-kiss-quotient-is-a-perfect-romantic-equation.

Sharma, Shivi. "Author Interview: 'Recipe for Persuasion' by Sonali Dev." *Brown Girl Magazine*, June 26, 2020. browngirlmagazine.com/2020/06/author-interview-recipe-for-persuasion-sonali-dev.

Dumpleton, Elise. "Q&A: Jane Igharo, Author of *Ties That Tether*." The Nerd Daily, September 26, 2020. www.thenerddaily.com/jane-igharo-author-interview.

Bryce, Denny S. "In *Get A Life, Chloe Brown*, Love Doesn't Cure All — But It Sure Is Fun." Book Review, National Public Radio, November 4, 2019. www.npr.org/2019/11/04/775207231/in-get-a-life-chloe-brown-love-doesnt-cure-all-but-it-sure-is-fun.

Arjini, Nawal. "Saeed Jones on Queer Masculinity and the Point of Being an Artist." *The Nation*, October 7, 2019. www.thenation.com/article/archive/saeed-jones-how-we-fight-for-our-lives-interview/.

Philyaw, Adira-Danique. "Guest Editor Morgan Rogers on *Honey Girl*." *She Reads*, February 1, 2021. shereads.com/guest-editor-morgan-rogers-on-honey-girl/.

Qasim, Noor. "Fantasy Is the Ultimate Queer Cliché: An Interview with Carmen Maria Machado." *The Paris Review*, November 5, 2019. www.theparisreview.org/blog/2019/11/05/fantasy-is-the-ultimate-queer-cliche-an-interview-with-carmen-maria-machado.

Vine, Betty. "Why You Should Totally Judge a Book by Its Cover: The Beautiful Art of Book Cover Design." *ARTpublika Magazine*, August 18, 2020. www.artpublikamag.com/post/why-you-should-totally-judge-a-book-by-its-cover-the-beautiful-art-of-book-cover-design.

Hendy, Vyki. "Samira Iravani on Creating the Cover for *Dig*." *Spine*, April 8, 2019. spinemagazine.co/articles/samira-iravani2

Diamond, Sarah. "We've Got This Covered: The Art of Book Jacket Design." Society of Children's Book Writers and Illustrators. Accessed February 17, 2021. www.scbwi.org/cover-design-feature.

León, Concepción. "Jason Reynolds Is on a Mission." *New York Times*, October 28, 2019. www.nytimes.com/2019/10/28/books/jason-reynolds-look-both-ways.html.

Reynolds, Jason "Write. Right. Rite" series. Library of Congress Research Guides. guides.loc.gov/jason-reynolds/grab-the-mic/wrr.

Ehrlich, Brenna. "*Firekeeper's Daughter*: Angeline Boulley's Book Headed to Netflix." *Rolling Stone*, March 16, 2021. rollingstone.com/culture/culture-features/firekeepers-daughter-book-angeline-boulley-netflix-higher-ground-obamas-1142727/.

Gerike, Lydia. "'Black joy is at the heart of' author and Indianapolis native Leah Johnson's YA novel." *IndyStar*, July 5, 2020.

"Transcript from an Interview with Kwame Alexander." Reading Rockets, WETA Public Broadcasting, March 22, 2016. www.readingrockets.org/books/interviews/alexander/transcript.

Lin, Grace. "The Windows and Mirrors of Your Child's Bookshelf." Produced by Brittany Horton. TED-Ed, TEDx talk, March 18, 2016. ed.ted.com/on/a0o0BODb.

Clare, Kerry. "Launchpad: *The Barren Grounds*, by David A. Robertson." 49th Shelf, September 28, 2020. 49thshelf.com/Blog/2020/09/28/Launchpad-THE-BARREN-GROUNDS-by-David-A.-Robertson.

Chang, Ailsa. "*Everything Sad Is Untrue* Is Funny and Sad and (Mostly) True." *All Things Considered*, National Public Radio, September 2, 2020. www.npr.org/2020/09/02/908467288/everything-sad-is-untrue-is-funny-and-sad-and-mostly-true.

Bird, Elizabeth. "The Pot Boileth Over: An Interview with Daniel Nayeri—A Fuse #8 Production." *School Library Journal*, August 19, 2020. blogs.slj.com/afuse8production/2020/08/19/daniel-nayeri-interview/.

Williams, Alicia D. *Genesis Begins Again*. New York: Atheneum/Caitlyn Dlouhy Books, 2020.
"A Visit with Bryan Collier | School Library Journal." *Mosaic Literary Magazine*, May 2, 2013. mosaicmagazine.org/a-visit-with-bryan-collier-school-library-journal.

Balaban, Samantha. "A New Picture Book Reminds Black Sons: *You Are Every Good Thing*." National Public Radio, October 24, 2020. www.npr.org/2020/10/24/925482149/a-new-picture-book-reminds-black-sons-you-are-every-good-thing.

Schu, John. "Your Name Is a Song by Jamilah Thompkins-Bigelow and Luisa Uribe." Watch. Connect. Read. (blog), October 1, 2019. mrschureads.blogspot.com/2019/10/your-name-is-song-by-jamilah-thompkins.html.

Tyner, Madeline. "The Numbers Are In: 2019 CCBC Diversity Statistics." CCBlogC, June 16, 2020. ccblogc.blogspot.com/2020/06/the-numbers-are-in-2019-ccbc-diversity.html.

Porter, Neal. "In Conversation: Yuyi Morales and Neal Porter." *Publishers Weekly*, August 16, 2018. www.publishersweekly.com/pw/by-topic/childrens/childrens-authors/article/77766-in-conversation-yuyi-morales-and-neal-porter.html.

Ayer, Bet. "The Groundbreaking Children's Books That Drew on Life in Thailand." Interview with Hannah Booth. *The Guardian*, June 17, 2017. www.theguardian.com/lifeandstyle/2017/jun/17/the-groundbreaking-childrens-books-that-drew-on-life-in-thailand.

Lodge, Sally. "Q & A with Kevin Noble Maillard and Juana Martinez-Neal." *Publishers Weekly*, October 17, 2019. www.publishersweekly.com/pw/by-topic/childrens/childrens-authors/article/81498-q-a-with-kevin-noble-maillard-and-juana-martinez-neal.html

"Meet the Illustrator: Christian Robinson." Brightly, May 27, 2015. www.readbrightly.com/meet-illustrator-christian-robinson.

"About Vashti Harrison." Accessed February 17, 2021. www.vashtiharrison.com/about.

Mora, Oge. "An Interview with Oge Mora." *Art of the Picture Book*, December 10, 2018. www.artofthepicturebook.com/-check-in with/2018/10/15/pm2gtdumqdmzg4qb8ffnwkgu9rbcc0.

"Juana Martinez-Neal." Full Circle Literary. Accessed February 17, 2021. www.fullcircleliterary.com/juana-martinez-neal.

Guzmán, Alicia Inez. "Red Planet Comics Is the Only Native Comic-Book Shop in the World." *New Mexico Magazine*, November 13, 2018. www.newmexico.org/nmmagazine/articles/post/red-planet-comics.

Associated Press. "Marvel Comic Book Aims to Improve Native American Portrayals." *Los Angeles Times*, August 31, 2020. www.latimes.com/entertainment-arts/story/2020-08-31/fans-hope-marvel-comic-book-improves-native-representation.

Sykes, Tanisha. "EyeSeeMe Bookstore Teaches Children the Value of African-American History." *USA Today*, April 10, 2019. www.usatoday.com/story/money/usaandmain/2019/04/10/eyeseeme-bookstore-black-history-children/2809180002.

Williams, Vonnie. "How Bryant Terry Is Decolonizing Vegan Cooking." Food52, February 25, 2020. food52.com/blog/25044-best-vegetable-kingdom-bryant-terry-cookbook-recipes.

"'I Can and I Will': The Best Acceptance Speeches Ever." *The Guardian*, October 8, 2015. www.theguardian.com/tv-and-radio/2015/oct/08/great-british-bake-off-nobel-prize-acceptance-speeches-nadiya-hussain.

Teigen, Chrissy, and Adeena Sussman. *Cravings*. New York: Clarkson Potter/Crown Publishing Group, February 2016.

Carter, Noelle. "Author Toni Tipton-Martin Takes Us Through the Rich History of African-American Cuisine." *Shondaland*, December 9 2019. www.shondaland.com/inspire/books/a30141244/toni-tipton-martin-interview.

Eby, Margaret. "Bryan Ford Is Leading a Sourdough Revolution." *Food & Wine*, June 18, 2020. www.foodandwine.com/bread-dough/bryan-ford-new-world-sourdough.

Sherman, Sean. "Interview with an Indigenous Chef: Sean Sherman." Interview by Molly Roe, Sweetgrass Trading Company (blog), July 1, 2020. www.sweetgrasstradingco.com/2020/07/01/interview-with-an-indigenous-chef-sean-sherman.

Gay, Roxane. "Be Bigger, Fight Harder: Roxane Gay on A Lifetime of 'Hunger.'" Interview with Terry Gross, *Fresh Air*, National Public Radio, June 19, 2017. www.npr.org/2017/06/19/533515895/be-bigger-fight-harder-roxane-gay-on-a-lifetime-of-hunger.

Díaz, Jaquira. "In New Memoir *Ordinary Girls*, Jaquira Díaz Searches for Home." Interview with Steve Inskeep. *Morning Edition*, National Public Radio, October 29, 2019. www.npr.org/2019/10/29/774306278/jaquira-d-az-on-her-memoir-ordinary-girls.

Lefaive, Ruth. "Zones of Paradox: A Conversation with Billy-Ray Belcourt." The Rumpus, July 15, 2020. therumpus.net/2020/07/the-rumpus-interview-with-billy-ray-belcourt.

Lurie, Julia. "Charles Blow on Masculinity, Trayvon Martin, and Reliving Childhood Trauma." *Mother Jones*, September/October 2014. www.motherjones.com/media/2014/09/interview-new-york-times-charles-blow-memoir-fire-shut-up-bones-trayvon-martin-masculinity.

Vinopal, Courtney. "Anacostia's First New Bookstore in 20 Years Hopes to Reflect the Diversity of Its Community." *Washingtonian*, December 20, 2017. www.washingtonian.com/2017/12/20/at-mahoganybooks-owners-derrick-and-ramunda-young-hope-to-reflect-the-diversity-of-their-community/.

"Meet Jhoanna Belfer of Bel Canto Books in Long Beach." Local Stories, *Voyage LA*, August 10, 2020. voyagela.com/interview/meet-jhoanna-belfer-bel-canto-books-long-beach/.

Aviles, Gwen. "In North Carolina, a Latino Bookstore and Cultural Hub Works to Survive Coronavirus Pandemic." *NBC News*, May 6, 2020. www.nbcnews.com/news/latino/north-carolina -latino-bookstore-cultural-hub-works-survive -coronavirus-pandemic-n1200496.

Reading Women. "Wayétu Moore on What It Means to Tell 'Our Story.'" Lithub, June 24, 2020. lithub.com/wayetu-moore-on-what-it-means-to -tell-our-story.

Brennan, Kailey. "Mira Jacob: On Family, Racism, Writing as a Lonely Art and Her Graphic Memoir, *Good Talk*." Write or Die Tribe, October 23, 2019. www.writeordietribe.com/author-interviews /interview-with-mira-jacob.

Goodwin, Connor. "Author Toni Jensen Reminds Us the Face of Gun Violence Is Not What We Think." *Shondaland*, September 8, 2020. www.shondaland.com/inspire/books/a33928495 /toni-jensen-carry-memoir.

Lorde, Audre. "I Am Your Sister: Black Women Organizing Across Sexualities," from *A Burst of Light*, reprinted in *Making Face, Making Soul / Haciendo Caras: Creative and Critical Perspectives by Feminists of Color*. Edited by Gloria Anzaldúa. San Francisco: Aunt Lute, September 1990.

Flood, Alison. "Rep John Lewis tells National Book Awards how he was refused entry to library because he was black." *The Guardian*, November 17, 2016. www.theguardian.com/books/2016/nov/17 /rep-john-lewis-national-book-awards-refused -entry-to-library-because-black.

Wilkerson, Isabel. "Great Migration: The African-American Exodus North." Interview with Terry Gross. *Fresh Air*, National Public Radio, September 13, 2010. www.npr.org/transcripts /129827444.

Chang, Juju, et al. "*Star Trek* star George Takei on why his activism roots are deeply personal and being a Twitter legend." *ABC News*, August 19, 2019. abcnews.go.com/Entertainment/star-trek-star-george -takei-activism-roots-deeply/story?id=64932887.

Miller, Kei. *Augustown*. New York: Vintage, 2018.

Diop, Arimeta. "Kimberly Drew and Jenna Wortham Look Toward the Future." *Vanity Fair*, November 17, 2020. www.vanityfair.com/style/2020/11/kimberly -drew-jenna-wortham-on-black-futures.

"*Black Futures*, by Kimberly Drew and Jenna Wortham: An Excerpt." *New York Times*, December 1, 2020. www.nytimes.com/2020/12/01 /books/review/black-futures-by-kimberly-drew -and-jenna-wortham-an-excerpt.html.

Kahn, Mattie. "Stacey Abrams Wants to Build a Better America. She Needs Your Help." *Glamour*, June 23, 2020. www.glamour.com/story/stacey -abrams-our-time-is-now-interview-2020-election.

Wong, Alice. "#ADA25: A Note of Gratitude from the DVP." Disability Visibility Project, July 27, 2015. disabilityvisibilityproject.com/2015/07/27/ada25 -dvp-a-note-of-gratitude.

Darden, Jenee. "Activist Alice Wong on the Joys and Challenges of Being Disabled." KALW Local Public Radio, September 10, 2020. www.kalw.org/post /activist-alice-wong-joys-and-challenges-being -disabled#stream/0.

Elie, Paul. "The Secret History of *One Hundred Years of Solitude*." *Vanity Fair*, December 9, 2015. www.vanityfair.com/culture/2015/12/gabriel-garcia -marquez-one-hundred-years-of-solitude-history.

Schuessler, Jennifer. "Ibram X. Kendi Has a Cure for America's 'Metastatic Racism.'" *New York Times*, August 6, 2019. www.nytimes.com/2019/08/06/arts /ibram-x-kendi-antiracism.html.

Kendi, Ibram X. Moreno, Nereida. "Historian Ibram X. Kendi on *How to Be An Antiracist*." Interview with Nereida Moreno, WBEZ Chicago, National Public Radio, October 30, 2019. www.npr.org/local/309/2019/10/30/774704183 /historian-ibram-x-kendi-on-how-to-be-an-antiracist.

McGhee, Heather. "*Sum of Us* Examines the Hidden Cost of Racism—For Everyone." Interview with Dave Davies, *Fresh Air*, National Public Radio, February 17, 2021. www.npr.org/2021/02/17 /968638759/sum-of-us-examines-the-hidden -cost-of-racism-for-everyone.

Egan, Elisabeth. "Heather McGhee Knows Readers Judge Books by Their Covers." *New York Times*, March 4, 2021. www.nytimes.com/2021/03/04/books/review/heather-mcghee-the-sum-of-us.html.

O'Rourke, Meghan. "Cathy Park Hong on *Minor Feelings*." *The Yale Review*, June 29, 2020. yalereview.yale.edu/cathy-park-hong-minor-feelings.

Perez, Lexy. "Author Austin Channing Brown on Lessons 'I Am Still Here' Memoir Teaches Amid Current Racial Justice Movement." *The Hollywood Reporter*, July 9, 2020. www.hollywoodreporter.com/news/i-am-still-here-author-austin-channing-brown-reflects-memoirs-success-1301731.

"About EJI." Equal Justice Initiative. Accessed January 18, 2021. www.facebook.com/equaljusticeinitiative/about/?ref=page_internal.

Coates, Ta-Nehisi. *Between the World and Me*. Ta-NehisiCoates.com. Accessed January 18, 2021. ta-nehisicoates.com/books/between-the-world-and-me.

Zavala-Offman, Alysa. "The Bibliophile: Janet Webster Jones, Source Booksellers Owner." The People Issue, *Detroit Metro Times*, August 9, 2017. www.metrotimes.com/detroit/the-bibliophile-janet-webster-jones/Content?oid=4902031.

Iron Dog Books. "5 Questions with Iron Dog Books." BookNet Canada, November 6, 2020. www.booknetcanada.ca/blog/2020/11/06/5-questions-with-iron-dog-books.

Harden, Brandon T. "Harriett's Bookshop Owner Hands Out Free Books about Black Leaders during Philly Marches." *Philadelphia Inquirer*, June 5, 2020. www.inquirer.com/arts/harrietts-bookshop-free-books-black-authors-fishtown-george-floyd-protests-20200605.html.

Ertem, Asli. "Confessions of a Bad Feminist." TEDxVienna, July 18, 2018. www.tedxvienna.at/blog/confessions-bad-feminist.

Hooks, Bell. *Feminism Is for Everybody: Passionate Politics*. New York: Routledge, 2014.

Hamad, Ruby. "Shelf Reflection: Ruby Hamad." *Kill Your Darlings*, October 11, 2019. www.killyourdarlings.com.au/article/shelf-reflection-ruby-hamad.

Chakraborty, Mridula Nath. "Ruby Hamad's damning assessment of race and feminism." *The Sydney Morning Herald*, September 13, 2019. www.smh.com.au/entertainment/books/ruby-hamads-damning-assessment-of-race-and-feminism-20190909-p52pcn.html.

Terrell, Kellee. "Mikki Kendall Reminds Us That Feminism Must Be for Everyone." *Shondaland*, February 25, 2020. www.shondaland.com/inspire/books/a31086399/mikki-kendall-hood-feminism.

Glass, Lelia. "Cherríe Moraga revisits her foundational book." The Clayman Institute for Gender Research, May 26, 2016. gender.stanford.edu/news-publications/gender-news/cherr-e-moraga-revisits-her-foundational-book.

Simon, Scott. "Samantha Irby: 'This Is the Glamorous Life of a Writer.'" *Weekend Edition Saturday*, National Public Radio, March 28, 2020. www.npr.org/2020/03/28/822561360/samantha-irby-this-is-the-glamorous-life-of-a-writer.

Calder, Tyler. "Samantha Irby on Her New Book, *Wow, No Thank You*." Girls' Night In, July 10, 2020. www.girlsnightin.co/posts/samantha-irby-on-making-friends-as-an-adult-book-club-snacks.

Sethi, Anita. "Esmé Weijun Wang: 'I don't want to glamorise mental illness . . . it inhibits creativity.'" *The Guardian*, June 29, 2019. www.theguardian.com/books/2019/jun/29/esme-weijun-wang-interview-the-collected-schizophrenias.

Tolentino, Jia. "Jia Tolentino." BookPage Interview with Jessica Wakeman. *BookPage*, August 2019. bookpage.com/interviews/24268-jia-tolentino-nonfiction#.YFpId_lKg2w.

Tolentino, Jia. "Jia Tolentino Knows We're F*cked—But Wants Us to Be Happy Anyway." Interview with Adrienne Westenfeld, *Esquire*, August 6, 2019, www.esquire.com/entertainment/books/a28607628/jia-tolentino-interview-trick-mirror/.

Bednar, Olivia. "The Best Independent Book Stores in Toronto." *NOW Magazine*, August 1, 2018. nowtoronto.com/culture/books-culture/best-independent-book-stores-toronto.

Parris, Amanda. "How A Different Booklist Changed Toronto (and Not Only through Books)." CBC, March 17, 2016. www.cbc.ca/arts/exhbitionists/how-a-different-booklist-changed-toronto-and-not-only-through-books-1.3496301.

Biersdorfer, J. D. "Where to Find Native American Culture and a Good Read." *New York Times*, July 25, 2019. www.nytimes.com/2019/07/25/books/birchbark-minneapolis-native-american-books.html.

Blakely, Lindsay. "The Co-Founder of L.A.'s Eso Won Books Reflects on Being a Black Man and Business Owner in the U.S." *Inc.*, September 3, 2020. www.inc.com/lindsay-blakely/eso-won-books-james-fugate-black-business-owner.html.

"7 Writers on Their Favorite Bookstores." *New York Times*, December 7, 2016. www.nytimes.com/interactive/2016/12/07/travel/7-authors-on-their-favorite-bookstores.html.

Atlas, Nava. "5 Things to Love about Gwendolyn Brooks." Literary Ladies Guide, August 17, 2017. www.literaryladiesguide.com/literary-musings/5-things-love-gwendolyn-brooks.

Barajas, Julia. "Who Is Amanda Gorman, Biden Inauguration Day Poet from L.A.?" *Los Angeles Times*, January 17, 2021. www.latimes.com/entertainment-arts/books/story/2021-01-17/amanda-gorman-biden-inauguration-poet.

"Fat, Fly & Brown." Yesikasalgado.com. Accessed February 3, 2021. www.yesikasalgado.com.

Reichard, Raquel. "This Poet's Words Are Exactly What You Need to Read If You're Getting Over a Breakup." Bustle, November 9, 2017. www.bustle.com/p/why-corazon-poet-yesika-salgado-wants-you-to-celebrate-your-heartbreaks-with-other-women-3258545.

Kaur, Rupi. *Milk and Honey*. Andrews McMeel Publishing. Accessed February 3, 2021. publishing.andrewsmcmeel.com/book/milk-and-honey/.

Prengel, Kate. "Joy Harjo: 5 Fast Facts You Need to Know." Heavy.com, June 20, 2019. heavy.com/news/2019/06/joy-harjo.

McGinnis, Laura. "Meet Alex Elle, the 27-Year-Old Writer Who's on a Mission to Empower Women to Love Themselves." NOMORE.org (blog), October 25, 2017. nomore.org/bloomstories-alex-elle.

Shacknai, Gabby. "Alex Elle Discusses Her New Book, the Fight to Democratize Wellness, and How to Make Self-Care a Part of Everyday Life." *Forbes*, September 30, 2020. www.forbes.com/sites/gabbyshacknai/2020/09/30/alex-elle-discusses-her-new-book-the-fight-to-democratize-wellness-and-how-to-make-self-care-a-part-of-everyday-life/?sh=66eb06de5a9e.

Ramírez, Alicia. "With *What Would Frida Do* Arianna Davis Finds Inspiration In an Acclaimed Feminist Icon." *Shondaland,* October 20, 2020. www.shondaland.com/inspire/books/a34417698/arianna-davis-what-would-frida-do/.

"My Grandmother's Hands." *Psychology Today*, September 21, 2017. www.psychologytoday.com/us/blog/the-author-speaks/201709/my-grandmother-s-hands.

Nezhukumatathil, Aimee. "When in Doubt, Smile Like an Axolotl." Lithub, September 11, 2020. lithub.com/when-in-doubt-smile-like-an-axolotl.

"How We Roll." The Lit. Bar. Accessed February 17, 2021. www.thelitbar.com/how-we-roll.

Hobbs, Ashley J. "Business Owner Noëlle Santos Is Not Backing Down." *Essence*, July 24, 2020. www.essence.com/news/money-career/noelle-santos-the-lit-bar-bookstore.